NO BALL

Chandramohan Puppala is a leading journalist and writer from Mumbai, India. He belongs to the first generation print journalists who has evolved in broadcast journalism as well.

Working with leading newspapers like *Indian Express, DNA, Mid Day* and for the newsrooms of Zee News, Star News, Star Majha, TV9 and Sakal he has developed into an all-round journalist. His vast experience of writing on organized crime, in-depth stories on parallel economy and the underbelly of Mumbai has earned him several accolades in the past. He has co-directed series on underworld and on the impact of tiger-crisis on the ecology of the Indian sub-continent.

NO BALL

The Murky World of Match Fixing

Chandramohan Puppala

PAN

This edition first published in India 2019 by Pan
an imprint of Pan Macmillan Publishing India Private Limited,
707, Kailash Building
26 K. G. Marg, New Delhi – 110 001
www.panmacmillan.co.in

Pan Macmillan, 20 New Wharf Road, London N1 9RR
Basingstoke and Oxford
Associated companies throughout the world
www.panmacmillan.com

ISBN 978-93-86215-91-8

1 3 5 7 9 8 6 4 2

Typeset by Manmohan Kumar
Printed and bound in India by
Gopsons Papers Ltd.

CONTENTS

PART II: A BRIEF HISTORY OF FIXING

PART III: THOSE WHO PULL THE STRINGS

A TIMELINE OF THE FIXED (1998–2018)

1998

Pakistan bowler Ata-ur-Rehman accuses Wasim Akram of offering him Rs 3 lakh to bowl poorly against New Zealand. As a result, Akram resigns as captain of the Pakistan team. Similarly, Rashid Latif accuses Akram, Salim Malik, Inzamam-ul-Haq, and Ijaz Ahmed of fixing matches. He also accuses Malik of fixing matches during Pakistan's twin tour of South Africa and Zimbabwe in 1994–95.

Mark Waugh, Shane Warne, and Tim May claim that Salim Malik offered them $ 50,000 to lose a Test during their tour to Pakistan in 1994. The Australian cricket board then asks the ICC to appoint a panel to look into the allegations. The PCB, in its inquiry, implicates three Pakistan players and recommends a ban on Salim Malik.

Shane Warne and Mark Waugh confess to having accepted $ 11,000 from an Indian bookie to give information on the playing conditions during a tournament played in Sri Lanka in 1994. The Australian cricket board later says it would impose a hefty fine on Warne and Waugh.

1999

Former England player Chris Lewis says he was offered £ 300,000 to persuade England players to lose a match against New Zealand.

2000

April 7: The Delhi Police charge Hansie Cronje with fixing South Africa's ODIs against India. They also reveal they are in possession of a conversation recorded during the ODI series between India and South Africa in March. They allege that the voices were of South African skipper Hansie Cronje and an Indian bookie, Sanjay Chawla. The conversation was about divulging team information and the amount to be paid to Cronje and his teammates, Herschelle Gibbs, Pieter Strydom, and Nicky Boje.

April 9: Hansie Cronje vehemently denies the charges levelled against him, saying, 'I have never received any sum of money for any match that I have been involved in and have never approached any of the players and asked them if they wanted to fix a game.'

April 11: The South African cricket board sacks Cronje after he calls Ali Bacher to confess that he was not entirely honest and admitted to having accepted $ 10,000–15,000 from a London-based bookmaker, but for forecasting results, not match-fixing.

April 15: Clouds of match-fixing surround England's victory in the Centurion Test, where Cronje took the unexpected step of forfeiting an innings.

April 16: It is revealed that South Africa nearly accepted $ 250,000 to lose an ODI against India, played at Mumbai in 1996. The players had discussed the offer in three meetings before it was turned down, as Jonty Rhodes, Dave Richardson, and Andrew Hudson were against it.

May 24: After a year-long inquiry, Justice Qayyum finds Salim Malik and Ata-ur-Rehman guilty of fixing matches and recommends life ban on the two. The report also says that Wasim Akram and Mushtaq Ahmed should not be allowed to captain Pakistan in the future.

June 7: On the first day of the King Commission hearings, former South African spinner Pat Symcox says that the team was offered around $ 250,000 to throw an ODI.

June 8: Herschelle Gibbs accuses Cronje of offering him a bribe to throw a match, and tells the King Commission that he had accepted Cronje's offer of $ 15,000 to score less than 20 runs in an ODI in India.

June 15: Cronje admits to taking money for giving information to bookmakers and asking his teammates to play badly. But he tells the King Commission that South Africa had never thrown or fixed a match under his captaincy.

June 27: Former commissioner of the Metropolitan Police, Sir Paul Condon, becomes the ICC's new anti-corruption investigator.

July 20: Indian income tax officials raid homes of top cricketers, including those of the then national coach Kapil Dev, and of former players, Mohammad Azharuddin, Ajay Jadeja, Nayan Mongia, and Nikhil Chopra.

August 28: South African cricket board bans Herschelle Gibbs and Henry Williams from international cricket for the rest of the year for their involvement in the Cronje scandal.

October 11: Cronje is banned from cricket for life by the UCBSA, as a result of his admission that he received money from bookmakers. 'The UCBSA council hereby intends to ban Hansie Cronje for life from all activities of the UCBSA and its affiliates,' says the statement.

October 31: Bookmaker M. K. Gupta names several players, including Brian Lara, Dean Jones, Alec Stewart, Arjuna Ranatunga, Aravinda de Silva, Martin Crowe, and Salim Malik for being involved in match-fixing, says a CBI report. The CBI also says that former Indian captain Mohammad Azharuddin confessed to fixing games with the help of colleagues Ajay Jadeja and Nayan Mongia.

November 27: BCCI's anti-corruption commissioner K. Madhavan finds Azharuddin guilty of match-fixing, while Ajay Jadeja, Manoj Prabhakar, Ajay Sharma, and former Indian team physio Ali Irani are found guilty of having links with bookies.

December 5: BCCI bans Azharuddin for life and Ajay Jadeja for five years for their role in match-fixing. Ajay Sharma is also banned from the game for life, while Prabhakar and Ali Irani are barred from holding any official post in Indian cricket for five years.

2001

July 11: Former England wicketkeeper-batsman Alec Stewart is cleared of allegations that he took money from a bookmaker in return for providing team and pitch information during England's 1992–93 tour of India.

2003

January 27: Delhi High Court overturns BCCI's ban imposed on Ajay Jadeja by saying there is no proof he was guilty.

December 22: Sri Lankan limited-overs team captain Marvan Atapattu comes under scrutiny, after an amount of $ 11,500 is found in the room occupied by him in Earl's Regency Hotel in Kandy during a Test match against England.

2004

May 12: Marvan Atapattu is cleared of match-fixing allegations by the ICC's Anti-Corruption unit for lack of evidence.

August 17: Kenyan player Maurice Odumbe is banned for five years by the Kenyan cricket association after he is found guilty of receiving money from bookmakers.

November 7: Stephen Fleming alleges that he was offered $ 370,000 during the 1999 World Cup to join a match-fixing syndicate.

2008

May 13: Marlon Samuels is banned for two years for allegedly passing on match-related information to an Indian bookie during the West Indies' ODI series in India in 2007.

2010

May 15: Essex cricketer Danish Kaneria and Mervyn Westfield are arrested, but not charged, in connection with alleged spot-fixing during Essex's Pro 40 against Durham. Both are released on bail until September 15, pending inquiry. Pakistan skipper Salman Butt, pacers Mohammad Asif and Mohammad Amir, wicketkeeper Kamran Akmal, and youngsters Umar Amin and Wahab Riaz come under the scanner for betting accusations.

August 28: *News of the World* reports that Mohammad Amir, Salman Butt, and Mohammad Asif were involved in spot-fixing during the fourth test-match against England at Lord's.

August 29: International cricket receives another major blow after bookie Mazhar Majeed reveals in a sting operation by *News of the World* that he bribed Pakistan bowlers to bowl no-balls on demand during the fourth Test.

September 2: International Cricket Council suspends Butt, Amir, and Asif.

2011

February 2: ICC bans Pakistan's tainted trio. Butt gets 10 years, of which five are suspended; Asif is banned for seven years, two suspended; and Amir docked five years.

November 3: A British Judge at London's Southwark Crown Court hands a thirty-month jail sentence to Butt, one year to Asif and six months to Amir for their part in the fixing scandal. Their corrupt British agent, Mazhar Majeed was given the longest sentence of thirty-two-months.

2012

February 1: Mohammad Amir is released from Portland Young Offenders Institution in Dorset after serving half of his six-month sentence.

May 3: Mohammad Asif is freed from Canterbury prison in Kent after six months into his twelve-month sentence.

June 21: Salman Butt is released from Canterbury prison after serving seven months of his thirty-month sentence. He was freed under the early prisoner-release scheme for foreigners, which usually is an agreement to be formally deported.

June 30: Indian trio Mohnish Mishra, Amit Yadav, and Abhinav Bali are banned for a year by the BCCI's disciplinary committee for bringing the game into disrepute, following an Indian TV sting operations. Shalabh Srivastava, also caught in the sting, is barred from cricket for five years after he is deemed guilty of agreeing and negotiating the terms to fix a match, though no fixing ultimately took place.

September 4: Ex-Bangladesh cricketer Shariful Haque is handed an indefinite suspension, after allegations of spot-fixing made by compatriot Mashrafe Mortaza are substantiated.

November 8: Andhra Pradesh High Court lifts life ban on Mohammad Azharuddin, terming it 'illegal'.

2013

May 15: Three bookies – Ramesh Vyas, Pandurang Kadam, and Ashok Vyas – are arrested by the Crime Branch. Later, another bookie, Pravin Behra, is held in Bhandup. All arrests are made in Mumbai.

May 16: Rajasthan Royals players S. Sreesanth, Ajit Chandila and Ankeet Chavan; Sreesanth's friend and alleged bookie Jiju Janardhan and 10 other bookies arrested. The special cell of the Delhi Police arrested Sreesanth from his friend's place in Mumbai while the other two cricketers were arrested the previous night from the team hotel at Nariman Point, Mumbai, for their alleged role in spot-fixing.

May 17: Former Rajasthan Royals and Gujarat pacer Amit Singh, also a bookie, is held by the Delhi Police. The three tainted players, along with Singh, are suspended by BCCI. All of them are charged by the police under Sections 420 (cheating) and 120-B (criminal conspiracy) of the IPC.

May 18: Ramesh, Vyas, and Kadam are linked to the spot-fixing scandal. Police search hotel rooms occupied by Sreesanth and Jiju Janardhan; seize a laptop, an iPad, a mobile phone and a diary of Sreesanth.

May 19: BCCI orders spot-fixing probe, appoints its anti-corruption chief and former IPS officer, Ravi Sawani, as the Commissioner of Inquiry. Rajasthan Royals files FIR against the tainted trio. The Sports Ministry consults with the Law Ministry to draft a new law to deal with betting in sports. Manish Budeywa, a former Ranji Trophy player, is picked up for questioning by the Delhi Police. Delhi Police asks hotels in Mumbai, Chandigarh, Kolkata, and Hyderabad to provide CCTV footage to scan meetings of the three arrested cricketers with bookies in connection with the IPL spot-fixing scandal.

May 20: Rajasthan Royals terminates the contract of Sreesanth, Chavan, and Chandila.

May 21: Bookie Prashanth is arrested in Chennai, confesses to organizing cricket betting in the city since the mid-'90s. Actor Vindoo Dara Singh is arrested for his alleged association with bookies. Former Ranji player Baburao Yadav from Vidarbha is arrested. The Supreme Court refuses to ban IPL, stating that it cannot be done just because of certain irregularities on the part of a few players. Bharat Petroleum Corporation Ltd suspends Sreesanth's contract. Sreesanth gives the first interview; claims innocence in the scandal.

May 23: A police team summons Chennai Super Kings Team Principal Gurunath Meiyappan for questioning. Pakistan umpire Asad Rauf probed by Mumbai Police and later withdrawn from the elite umpires' panel for the ICC Champions Trophy 2013. Income tax department initiates a probe into the *hawala* and illegal cash transactions involved in the spot-fixing.

May 24: After questioning, Meiyappan arrested by Mumbai Police on charges of betting, conspiracy, and cheating. BCCI officials meet Kapil Sibal, demanding anti-fixing law.

May 25: India Cements issues statement that Meiyappan is not the owner or team principal of CSK. Lalit Modi demands the termination of CSK from IPL. BCCI President and CSK's de facto owner, N. Srinivasan rejects demands for his resignation. Tainted Rauf dropped from ICC Elite Panel. Mumbai Police describe Meiyappan as being 'non-cooperative' and 'evasive' during interrogation.

May 26: BCCI suspends Meiyappan, pending inquiry, and announces three-member commission to investigate him.

Meiyappan booked under various sections of the IT Act, Gambling Act, and the Indian Penal Code. Meiyappan said that he was coaxed to place bets by Vindoo. Admits to having passed on vital information on the team's strategy to the bookies through Vindoo. Mumbai Police jointly question Meiyappan and Vindoo. Sreesanth and three others are sent to two-day police custody by Delhi High Court. Three-man commission consisting of Justice T. Jayarama Chouta, Justice R. Balasubramanian and BCCI secretary Sanjay Jagdale, appointed to look into the charges of betting.

May 27: BCCI President N. Srinivasan alleges his resignation sought only by a 'hounding media'.

May 28: S. Sreesanth sent to judicial custody. M. S. Dhoni keeps mum on the spot-fixing episode

May 29: A Mumbai High court extends police custody of Meiyappan. Umpire Rauf says ready for a probe by ICC.

May 30: Ankeet Chavan granted bail to get married, made to deposit two sureties of Rs 1 lakh each and a personal bond of Rs 1 lakh before release.

May 31: CB-CID raid accused, Chennai-based Vikram Aggarwal's hotels (Radisson Blu and Fortune Palm). Police custody of Meiyappan, Vindoo extended till June 3. RR player Trivedi to be a prosecution witness in IPL case. Secretary Sanjay Jagdale and treasurer Ajay Shirke submit their resignation in protest against N. Srinivasan's refusal to quit. Chavan released from Tihar Jail.

June 1: Rajiv Shukla resigns from the post of IPL Chairman.

June 2: Srinivasan steps aside, Dalmiya named interim-president – N. Srinivasan agreed to "step aside" as BCCI President under a compromise formula that brought back former chief Jagmohan Dalmiya as head of a four-member "interim arrangement" to run the Board.

June 4: Meiyappan, Vindoo and six bookies are granted bail on a bond of Rs 25,000 each. Delhi Police invokes Maharashtra Control of Organised Crime Act (MCOCA) provisions against Sreesanth & Co. to strengthen the case against those involved in the IPL spot-fixing saga, claiming bookies like Ashwini Aggarwal were working at the behest of Dawood gang. Sreesanth moves fresh bail application before a Delhi court after police invoke MCOCA against him and others.

June 5: Rajasthan Royals owner Raj Kundra is questioned by Delhi Police. BCCI's Commissioner of Inquiry, Sawani submits IPL spot-fixing internal probe report to BCCI without getting any access to the arrested players and complete evidence collected by the Delhi Police.

June 6: Police file charges against Raj Kundra for admitting to betting on his own team during IPL matches.

June 10: Kundra suspended by the BCCI on charges of gambling during IPL 6 matches. BCCI anti-corruption chief Sawani's report on the spot-fixing scam is forwarded to the Board's disciplinary panel in an emergent Working Committee Meeting. A Delhi court grants bail to Sreesanth, Ankeet Chavan and 18 others on a personal bond of Rs 50,000, stating there is prima facie "no sufficient material" against the accused to establish their "nexus" with an organized crime syndicate.

June 11: Sreesanth and Chavan released from Tihar on bail. Sreesanth continues to maintain innocence saying he was confident of getting a clean chit and hopeful of making a return to the national side.

June 12: Hearing on the bail pleas of Rajasthan Royals' Ajit Chandila and four others deferred by a Delhi court, which remanded bookie Sunil Bhatia to two-day police custody.

June 13: In reply to a PIL seeking transfer of the probe by Delhi and Mumbai police to the CBI, to unearth a larger conspiracy and insulate the investigation from highly influential persons and politicians, the Supreme Court says no trouble with separate probes, by Delhi Police and it counterparts in Mumbai in the case.

June 14: The Delhi Police opposes the bail plea of Chandila, saying he is a "key conspirator" in the entire case and was acting at the behest of a syndicate run by gangster Dawood Ibrahim.

June 17: Chandila remanded to fresh police custody for three days by a Delhi court, requiring him to corroborate evidence collected from other accused after invoking MCOCA.

June 20: Former IPL commissioner Lalit Modi claims that three Chennai Super Kings players had links with a real-estate tycoon, who is also a bookie and has close links with Gurunath Meiyappan and other IPL franchise owners.

June 21: The Cricket Association of Bihar files a PIL in the Bombay High Court against the constitution of the probe panel by then BCCI chief N. Srinivasan, alleging it was an 'exercise' to 'cover up' the activities of his son-in-law, Gurunath Meiyappan.

June 24: BCCI Anti-corruption Chief Sawani grills Sreesanth for three hours.

July 5: The Mumbai Police arrests big-time bookie Shobhan Mehta in connection with the IPL betting case after picking up him from Goa. The number of arrests in the case goes up to 17.

July 6: Rajasthan Royals left-arm spinner Harmeet Singh appears before Sawani and is questioned for close to one-and-a-half hour in the spot-fixing probe. Harmeet claims Chandila and the bookies urged him to indulge in spot-fixing but he said no. He also says that Chandila was approached by three bookies to rope in Shane Watson. BCCI suspends him for not reporting the incident because it amounts to a breach of BCCI's anti-corruption code.

July 13: PCB drops Rauf from the list recommended for ICC umpires' panels.

July 16: Rahul Dravid to act as a prosecution witness in IPL spot-fixing case.

July 17: Audio intercepts of telephone calls played by the Delhi Police in a Delhi court to buttress its claim about the nexus between underworld don Dawood Ibrahim and bookies in the IPL spot-fixing scandal.

July 28: Two-judge probe panel constituted by the BCCI find no evidence against BCCI President-in-exile N. Srinivasan's team Chennai Super Kings in the IPL spot-fixing and betting scandal.

July 30: Bombay HC demands fresh probe against Meiyappan and Kundra; declares the Board's probe panel illegal and unconstitutional, questions the logic of the report finding everyone innocent despite not even speaking to the police. Delhi Police seek cancellation of Sreesanth and Chavan's bail. Sreesanth charge-sheeted along with Dawood & Co.

August 1: Niranjan Shah calls for fresh spot-fixing probe panel.

August 2: Fearing legal trouble after the Bombay High Court declared its IPL spot-fixing probe "illegal and unconstitutional", the under-fire Board calls off its Working Committee meeting in New Delhi. BCCI secretary Sanjay Patel clarifies that "a slight mistake" in the circular issued to summon the Working Committee Meeting in Delhi forced it to be called off.

August 3: Rauf reportedly retires from all forms of umpiring.

August 4: Chandila claims innocence in the IPL spot-fixing episode and says the Delhi Police's decision to slap the stringent Maharashtra Control of Organised Crime Act (MCOCA) charges against him is completely unfair, as he is a "cricketer and not a terrorist". Chandila granted an interim bail for two days (from August 3 to 5) to attend the last rites of his elder brother.

August 5: BCCI moves Supreme Court over Bombay HC ruling on IPL probe panel.

August 7: The Supreme Court refuses to grant interim stay on the Bombay High Court order, declaring the BCCI's two-member probe panel illegal and unconstitutional.

September 7: Mumbai Police names Meiyappan in its charge sheet filed before a Mumbai Court.

September 9: Ajit Chandila is granted bail by a Delhi court. Others are also granted bail over a passage of time.

September 13: BCCI hands out life ban to Sreesanth and Chavan, while Amit Singh is banned for five years, and Siddharth Trivedi for a year. No decision is taken on Chandila, who is yet to depose before Sawani.

October 1: Mike Hussey writes in his book *Underneath the Southern Cross* that Meiyappan and Kepler Wessels run CSK. 'Our owner was Indian Cements, headed by Mr Srinivasan,' Hussey wrote in his autobiography. 'As he was also on the board of the BCCI, he gave control of the team to his son-in-law Mr Gurunath. He ran the team along with Kepler Wessels, who was the coach.'

October 7: The Supreme Court appoints a three-member committee headed by former Punjab and Haryana High Court chief justice Mukul Mudgal, additional solicitor general N. Nageshwar Rao and Assam Cricket Association member Nilay Dutta. The committee is given four months to investigate IPL corruption charges.

October 14: Hussey does a U-turn. 'Certainly, Guru was around the team a lot. I knew he was talking to Kepler (Wessels, Super Kings' coach in IPL 2008) and the players, and we saw him at training and at the hotel. I didn't know what his official title was but he was around the team quite often. I probably may have written the wrong thing,' he was quoted as saying.

November 6: The Mudgal panel meets BCCI Anti-Corruption and Security chief Ravi Sawani and Mumbai Joint Commissioner of Police Himanshu Roy.

November 15–17: The Mudgal panel meets IPL COO Sundar Raman, former BCCI vice-president Chirayu Amin, Chavan, Sreesanth, Harmeet Singh, Kundra, and Vindoo.

November 18: Delhi Police file 1000-page supplementary charge sheet referring to the intercepted telephonic conversation between bookie Chandresh Jain alias Jupiter, and Salman alias Master, who belonged to the underworld.

December 5: Mudgal panel meets Chandila and Siddharth Trivedi.

December 19: Srinivasan meets the Mudgal Committee but Meiyappan doesn't and sends a letter instead of exercising his right to remain silent and "not affect his right to defend himself in the criminal case".

2014

January 4: The Mudgal panel meets former BCCI president IS Bindra, lawyer Rahul Mehra, former IPL Governing Council chairman Rajeev Shukla, BCCI vice-president Arun Jaitley and others.

January 19–20: The Mudgal panel meets former BCCI president Jagmohan Dalmiya, former Indian captain Sourav Ganguly and 'stakeholders' in Bangalore.

February 10: After meeting 100 people and more in nearly four months, the Mudgal Panel presents a report to the Supreme Court. The judges have been given a single copy of a sealed envelope whose contents are available only for the Court. The envelope will only be opened and its contents read by the judges. Justice Mudgal tells the media that Meiyappan was the face of Chennai

Super Kings and the team official of CSK. Meiyappan had been in violations of several sections of the IPL Operational Rules, the IPL Anti-Corruption Code and Articles of the Code of Conduct for Players and team officials. Kundra, the Rajasthan Royals team owner, had resorted to betting in the IPL through Umesh Goenka is 'evident' from Goenka's statements recorded by a Delhi court. The question of whether Meiyappan was involved in match-fixing and spot-fixing had not been investigated thoroughly by the anti-corruption units of the ICC and the BCCI or the Crime Branch Criminal Investigation Department of the Chennai Police, even though some information was available for such an investigation to be conducted.

March 7: Supreme Court adjourns taking up arguments until March 25, since it had not read the Justice Mudgal Committee's reports yet.

March 18: CSK and India skipper M. S. Dhoni file a Rs 100-crore defamation case in the Madras High Court against media houses Zee Media Corporation and News Nation Network for linking him with illegal activities of betting, match-fixing, and spot-fixing.

March 25: The Supreme Court suggests that Srinivasan step down to enable fair investigation into the allegations of betting. 'It's nauseating that N. Srinivasan continues as BCCI chief, he should go if cricket has to be cleaned,' the apex court observes. Srinivasan refused to comment, saying he would study the Court observations.

March 27: The Supreme Court proposes that former Indian captain Sunil Gavaskar should take over as the interim chief of the BCCI in place of its embattled president N. Srinivasan. It also suggests that Chennai Super Kings and Rajasthan Royals should not be allowed to take part in IPL and no person associated with India Cements should be involved with the BCCI.

March 28: N. Srinivasan, the head of the Board of Control for Cricket in India, is removed by the Supreme Court. The BCCI proposes that its secretary Sanjay Patel will run the board in Srinivasan's absence. It also requests the SC not to curtail Srinivasan's 'hefty role' in international cricket.

May 31: Court orders property attachment of Dawood, Chhota Shakeel, Pakistan-based Javed Chautani, Salman alias Master, and Ehteysham.

April 20: The BCCI suggests a three-man committee to SC to probe IPL scandal. The BCCI decided to suggest names of former Indian allrounder Ravi Shastri, former Calcutta High Court chief justice J. N. Patel, and ex-CBI director R. K. Raghavan as members of the probe committee.

April 22: The SC asks the Justice Mudgal Committee to investigate the IPL corruption issue, and in particular, the 13 names mentioned in the sealed envelope, with the assistance of other investigators. Mudgal has communicated to the court his willingness to take up the investigation and has been asked to specify the terms and modalities on April 29, the next date of hearing.

April 29: The BCCI says it wants the SC to form a new panel as it had found the Mudgal Committee's report "erroneous". At the hearing, the BCCI counsel also asked the court to reinstate

Srinivasan to his office as BCCI president while the probe was being conducted.

May 16: The SC empowers Justice Mudgal to head the investigation into the IPL and asks him to look into the 'sealed envelope'. Apart from Mudgal, L. Nageswara Rao, Nilay Dutta, and former IPS officer B. B. Mishra are also in the probe panel.

May 22: The Supreme Court declines Srinivasan's plea to be reinstated as the BCCI president for non-IPL affairs. The court rules that it will not interfere with an earlier order that had asked Srinivasan to stand aside as board chief for the duration of the investigation into alleged corruption in the IPL.

June 8: It is announced that Sourav Ganguly will join the Mudgal-led committee that is probing allegations of corruption in the IPL on Justice Mudgal's request, including the investigation of 13 individuals listed in a sealed envelope that was given to the SC after a preliminary inquiry.

June 12: The SC allows Srinivasan to contest for the top ICC post by declining an injunction petition from the Cricket Association of Bihar.

June 18: Star batsman Mohammad Ashraful banned for eight years (three years suspended) by the Bangladesh Premier League anti-corruption tribunal for his involvement in match and spot-fixing in the 2013 BPL. Sri Lanka's Kaushal Lokuarachchi is also banned for eighteen months for the same offence.

June 26: N Srinivasan confirmed as the Chairman of the ICC after the fifty-two-member Full Council approves amendments to the

ICC's Memorandum and Articles of Association at the Annual Conference in Melbourne.

July 1: New Zealand batsman Lou Vincent admits he was involved in match-fixing on many occasions while playing in the English county. The England and Wales Cricket Board, while imposing a lifetime ban on Vincent, says the Kiwi player pleaded guilty to eighteen breaches of its anti-corruption code.

July 18: Supreme Court relieves Sunil Gavaskar as interim president of BCCI – IPL affairs and appoints board Vice-President, Shivlal Yadav, to continue in the interim capacity as chief of BCCI for all non-IPL related matters.

August 29: The Mudgal Committee submits an interim report to the Supreme Court.

September 1: The Mudgal Committee gets a two-month extension for its final report. The SC also refuses to reinstate Srinivasan pending an inquiry.

September 29: Former Bangladesh captain Mohammad Ashraful's eight-year ban is reduced to five years (two years suspended) by the Bangladesh Cricket Board's disciplinary panel Chairman Justice Mohammad Abdur Rashid, following an appeal by the player.

September 30: Court declares Dawood, Chhota Shakeel and Chandigarh-based Sandeep Sharma as proclaimed offenders.

November 3: The Mudgal Committee submits its final report in the IPL corruption case to the Supreme Court, which will take it up on November 10. The report could determine, among other things, whether ICC Chairman Srinivasan can seek re-election as president of the BCCI.

November 10: The SC takes up the multiple reports submitted by the Mudgal Committee and postpones the hearing until November 14. The apex court asks the BCCI why the report cannot be made public.

November 11: Bombay High Court squashes the conflict-of-interest PIL against Srinivasan, filed by the Cricket Association of Bihar chief, challenging two amendments brought out by the BCCI in its rules, allegedly to favour Srinivasan.

November 17: Supreme Court slams Srinivasan, says no distinction between BCCI and IPL.

November 18: The BCCI calls the allegations against N. Srinivasan 'baseless' and gives him a clean chit in the IPL corruption case after reviewing the contents of the Mudgal report in the Working Committee Meeting. The working committee also decides to back Sundar Raman after hearing out his explanations.

November 21: Srinivasan seeks reinstatement as BCCI chief.

November 24: Conflict of interest returns to haunt Srinivasan in the Supreme Court.

November 25: The SC says Meiyappan's role in IPL scam is like insider trading.

November 27: The SC throws suggestions that those named in the Mudgal Committee could be kept out of BCCI elections and the CSK franchise could be scrapped.

December 1: The SC says the onus of disproving conflict of interest is on Srinivasan.

December 9: The SC proposes a high-powered committee to cleanse cricket.

December 10: Srinivasan agrees to keep away from the IPL, seeks an SC nod for reinstatement as BCCI president.

December 15: The SC decides to examine a controversial amendment in the BCCI rules, which enables office bearers to own teams in the IPL and Champions League T20, amidst a raging debate over the conflict-of-interest issue. It also slams IPL Chief Operating Officer Sundar Raman for not taking any action even though he was aware that officials were involved in betting.

December 17: The SC asks players and administrators with interests not to run the game and reserves order in the alleged betting and spot-fixing scam case.

2015

January 22: The SC bars Srinivasan from standing for any post in the BCCI. It sets up a committee, comprising former chief justice of India RM Lodha, former justice Ashok Bhan and former justice R. Raveendran to determine appropriate punishments for Meiyappan, Kundra and their respective franchises. The apex court strikes down Rule 6.2.4 of the BCCI constitution, which allowed board officials to own a team. BCCI told to hold elections in the next six weeks.

May 23: Court reserves order on framing of charges.

July 11: The three-member panel says it will announce the quantum of punishment on July 14 for Meiyappan, Kundra and the teams they were part of – CSK and Rajasthan Royals respectively – for their alleged involvement in the IPL 2013 corruption scandal.

July 14: Chennai Super Kings and Rajasthan Royals are suspended for two years by the Supreme Court-appointed Justice Lodha Committee. Former CSK team official Gurunath Meiyappan and Rajasthan Royals co-owner Raj Kundra are also suspended for life from BCCI-related activity.

July 25: All the 36 accused are discharged, including Sreesanth, Chandila, and Chavan, by the Delhi High Court.

November 9: Retired Justice A. P. Shah is appointed as Ombudsman of BCCI during its 86th Annual General Meeting. BCCI President Shashank Manohar to replace N. Srinivasan as ICC Chairman; Indian Team Director Ravi Shastri dropped from IPL governing council and selector Roger Binny, whose son Stuart is in contention for a place in the national team, is axed to avoid conflict of interest barbs. Six new venues – Visakhapatnam, Ranchi, Indore, Pune, Dharamsala, and Rajkot – are accorded Test status. Rajeev Shukla, Jyotiraditya Scindia, Ajay Shirke, M. P. Pandove and Sourav Ganguly form the modified five-member IPL governing council, which earlier had twenty-three members.

2016

January 4: Lodha panel submits their recommendations to the apex court to overhaul the functioning of the BCCI. These recommendations comprise: age cap of seventy years for office bearers, cooling-off period after one term, the appointment of a Comptroller and Auditor General (CAG) official for the board, no ad-breaks during IPL, the appointment of CEO and CFO to the board, one-state-one-vote policy, etc.

January 7: BCCI President Anurag Thakur asks state associations to study the Lodha report through an e-mail and gave the boards a deadline of January 31 to respond on how it affected them individually.

January 25: Gulam Bodi banned for 20 years by Cricket South Africa after he admitted to contriving or attempting to fix matches during the 2015 Ram Slam T20 series.

February 4: The SC sets a deadline of March 3 for the board to respond to the Lodha reforms and say they find no reason to disagree with the recommendations of the committee.

February 5: BCCI President Anurag Thakur makes it clear that the board needs time to go over a report as big as the one prepared by the Lodha panel. Two days later, the board calls an SGM to discuss the Lodha panel reforms at length.

February 19: BCCI comes up with a list of 'difficulties' in the implementation of the reforms and also points out 'anomalies' that make the reforms practically unimplementable. The BCCI president is asked to file an affidavit in the SC to counter Lodha panel's reforms. However, the board agrees on the appointment of a chief executive officer (CEO) and a chief financial officer (CFO).

March 1: BCCI files an affidavit in the Supreme Court challenging the Lodha panel reforms.

March 3: The SC questions BCCI for showing resistance to one-state-one-vote suggestion.

April 5: The SC lambasts BCCI for their funds' allocation policy and irrational distribution of funds to the affiliated states.

April 8: The SC also opposes BCCI's idea that any judicial intervention in its day-to-day operations would undermine their autonomy.

April 19: The SC comes down heavily on the suggestion that the one-state-one-vote recommendation would lead to politics within the BCCI.

April 20: Rahul Johri appointed as the CEO of BCCI.

April 29: SC is not ready to buy BCCI's suggestion that the age-cap of their office-bearers should be 70.

May 2: The SC makes it clear that the BCCI and all of its state associations will have to implement the Lodha reforms and a day later says that the board's constitution is incapable of achieving the values of transparency, objectivity, and accountability and that it needed to be changed.

July 18: The Supreme Court tightens the noose around the Indian cricket board by accepting a majority of the reforms suggested by the Lodha panel and gives the board a time frame of four-to-six months to implement the same.

July 21: The Lodha panel makes its stance clear on the nine-year cap for administrators in state boards, says that those who have completed nine years in the job cumulatively cannot contest for another term.

July 24: Former BCCI president Sharad Pawar says he will step down from the position of Mumbai Cricket Association president in light of the Lodha panel reforms.

August 2: BCCI sets up a new legal panel to interact with the Lodha Committee and appoints former Supreme Court judge Markandey Katju to head the panel.

August 7: Justice Katju stirs a hornet's nest by calling SC's July 18 order asking BCCI to implement Lodha panel reforms as "unconstitutional and illegal".

August 8: Former South African Test wicketkeeper Thami Tsolekile is banned for twelve years by Cricket South Africa for contriving to fix matches in the 2015 Ram Slam T20 Series. Three other cricketers, Jean Symes (seven years), Ethy Mbhalati, and Pumelela Matshikwe (ten years each), are also banned for breaching the anti-corruption code during the T20 series.

August 9: The Lodha panel sets September 30 as the deadline for the implementation of the first phase of the reforms. BCCI secretary Ajay Shirke meets the Lodha Committee and says the board will follow the timelines.

August 16: BCCI files a review petition against the July 18 SC judgment.

August 22: BCCI announces to hold its Annual General Meeting (AGM) on September 21. But the Lodha panel also makes it clear that it will be illegal if the recommendations are not adopted.

August 31: Lodha panel asks the BCCI to form a new IPL governing council by December 30.

September 12: ICC CEO Dave Richardson says BCCI President Anurag Thakur had asked the global body to send a letter to clarify that the Lodha panel reforms did not amount to government interference in the running of the board.

September 21: BCCI appoints M. S. K. Prasad as the Chief of the five-member National Selection Committee during the AGM. The Lodha panel had recommended to reduce it to three members. BCCI ends ombudsman, retired Justice AP Shah's one-year tenure, two months in advance.

September 28: Lodha Committee, in a scathing status report, tells the SC that the BCCI had created 'impediments' in the implementation of reforms and recommends that all existing office-bearers of the board be replaced by a caretaker panel of administrators.

September 30: BCCI misses the first deadline set for September 30, and also fails to adopt the Memorandum of Association and Rules and Regulations at its SGM. Contrary to their parent body, Vidarbha and Tripura accept Lodha recommendations in toto.

October 1: BCCI agrees to implement certain reforms but ignores the contentious ones like age-restriction of 70 years for board officials, the tenure-cap of nine years with cooling-off periods, and the one-state-one-vote policy.

October 3: Yes Bank and Bank of Maharashtra asked by Lodha Committee not to disburse funds from the BCCI accounts to the state associations.

October 7: The SC, in an interim order, says no money should be given to state associations until Lodha Committee recommendations are accepted. It asks President Anurag Thakur to submit a personal affidavit clarifying whether he had sought ICC intervention against the implementation of the Lodha panel recommendations.

October 15: The board fails to get two-thirds majority among the member associations for implementing the Lodha recommendations in totality.

October 17: The SC reserves order on the judgment in the case.

October 18: Hearing of BCCI's review petition of the July 18 verdict is adjourned.

October 21: The SC directs BCCI not to disburse funds to state associations until they accept the Lodha reforms.

November 21: The Lodha Committee proposes to the apex court that all BCCI and state association office bearers who do not satisfy the approved criteria be 'disqualified' with immediate effect.

December 2: BCCI continues to defy the Lodha reforms in their Special General Meeting (SGM).

December 15: The Supreme Court says BCCI President Anurag Thakur has committed perjury and could be arrested if allegations are proved. Thakur, SC claimed, had filed a false affidavit with regards to his communication with the ICC.

December 21: Former South African opener Alviro Petersen banned for two years by Cricket South Africa over breaches of the anti-corruption code, in relation to match-fixing during a domestic T20 competition in the 2015–16 season.

2017

January 2: Anurag Thakur and Ajay Shirke are removed from their posts of president and secretary of BCCI respectively by the Supreme Court, for not complying with the orders of the apex court in implementing the Lodha Committee reforms. The

SC also orders the formation of a Committee of Administrators (CoA) to oversee the business operations of the BCCI.

January 24: The BCCI asked to submit its own list of names for office bearers in a sealed envelope by January 27.

January 30: The SC appoints former comptroller and auditor general of India, Vinod Rai as head of BCCI's four-member Committee of Administrators (CoA), to run the affairs of BCCI. It includes noted historian and writer Ramachandra Guha, former women's cricket team captain Diana Edulji and Vikram Limaye, Managing Director and CEO of Infrastructure Development Finance Corporation (IDFC).

February 10: Islamabad United batsmen Sharjeel Khan and Khalid Latif are provisionally suspended following an investigation by the Pakistan Cricket Board in the 2017 Pakistan Super League in the UAE. Both players are sent home.

June 1: Ramachandra Guha resigns from the CoA and, in a scathing resignation letter, blames the 'superstar culture' in Indian cricket for his disillusionment with the sport and its administration. He also states that the CoA has not been able to perform the task that was given to them by the Supreme Court.

June 11: Vinod Rai says fellow CoA member Vikram Limaye will be stepping down on July 14 following his appointment as Managing Director and CEO of National Stock Exchange.

July 12: CoA complains to the Supreme Court in its fourth status report, that N. Srinivasan and Niranjan Shah are creating impediments in the implementation of Lodha reforms.

July 13: Ousted BCCI president Anurag Thakur issues an unconditional apology to the Supreme Court with regards to the perjury case against him.

July 14: The Supreme Court issues notices to Srinivasan and Shah, based on the CoA's fourth status report. The SC accepts Thakur's apology and drops the perjury charges against him.

July 24: Srinivasan and Shah are barred by the SC from attending BCCI SGM scheduled for July 26. It also states that the one-state-one-vote order will be looked into, as it might not be good for Indian cricket.

July 26: The BCCI, at its Special General Meeting, adopts Lodha panel reforms partially, rejecting all major recommendations on good governance, including age cap, tenure and a cooling-off period.

August 15: In its fifth status report, the CoA accuses the BCCI of misinterpreting the Supreme Court order to keep BCCI CEO Rahul Johri and the legal team out of the SGM. It also asks the Supreme Court to remove the BCCI top brass for failing to implement Lodha reforms.

August 23: The Supreme Court of India issues show-cause notice to BCCI's acting-president C. K. Khanna, secretary Amitabh Choudhary and treasurer Anirudh Chaudhry, to explain why the Lodha Committee recommendations have not been implemented. The apex court also asks the CoA to make a new draft of the BCCI constitution and place it in front of the bench.

August 30: Pakistan Cricket Board's anti-corruption tribunal bans Sharjeel Khan for five years (two-and-a-half years suspended) for his role in a spot-fixing scandal in the 2017 Pakistan Super League.

September 11: CoA submits a draft of BCCI constitution to the Supreme Court.

September 20: Pakistan Cricket Board finds Khalid Latif guilty of breaching its anti-corruption code during the 2017 PSL and is banned for five years.

September 21: The Supreme Court orders BCCI to make suggestions on the draft constitution.

October 30: A draft constitution of the BCCI is submitted in the Supreme Court, incorporating suggestions of the Lodha panel reforms. The court decides to hear BCCI's suggestions on November 29.

November 29: The SC adjourns BCCI draft constitution hearing to the second week of January 2018. The apex court also seeks a response from BCCI treasurer Anirudh Chaudhry, after taking note of an allegation that he had threatened the Board's Chief Financial Officer (CFO) Santosh Rangnekar.

December 11: Batsman Nasir Jamshed banned for a year by the Pakistan Cricket Board for failing to cooperate in the 2017 Pakistan Super League spot-fixing scandal.

2018

January 24: The CoA, in its sixth status report to the Supreme Court, indicts BCCI treasurer Anirudh Choudhary for stalling the implementation of Lodha reforms. The report also sought directions from the apex court on the appointment of an ombudsman, approval of the new conflict of interest rules and reconstitution of the steering committee to decide upon the cricket players' association.

March 8: The CoA, through its seventh status report, requests the Supreme Court to remove the current set of BCCI office-bearers, citing the end of their tenures. It also asks the SC to issue directions to convene the 88th Annual General Meeting of the BCCI, appoint an election officer and conduct the elections.

July 2: CoA flays the BCCI's acting secretary for not signing the player contracts in its ninth status report. The Indian cricket team leaves on England tour without the contracts.

August 9: Supreme Court approves new BCCI constitution, drawn up by the CoA, based on recommendations of the Lodha Committee, with key tweaks. Among the Lodha recommendations that do not find favour in the current constitution is the one-state-one-vote policy and the cooling-off period for office-bearers after one term. The removal of one-state-one-vote policy means all the associations based in Maharashtra and Gujarat – Vidarbha, Mumbai and Saurashtra, and Baroda – will retain their full membership in the BCCI while the cooling-off period will be after two consecutive three-year terms in office.

August 17: PCB bans Nasir Jamshed for 10 years after an independent anti-corruption tribunal comprising retired judge Fazal-E-Miran Chauhan, cricketer Aaqib Javed and Supreme Court advocate Shazaib Masood finds him guilty of five breaches of PCB's anti-corruption code.

September 12: The Tamil Nadu Cricket Association petitions the Supreme Court to dissolve the SC-appointed Committee of Administrators for having "acted contrary to the mandate of orders passed by this Hon'ble court."

October 13: BCCI CEO Rahul Johri is accused of inappropriate behaviour by author Harnidh Kaur through her twitter handle @pedestrianpoet. CoA demands an explanation from Johri about the same.

October 15: Sri Lankan legend Sanath Jayasuriya is charged by the International Cricket Council for breaching its anti-corruption code on two counts. The charges relate to Jayasuriya not cooperating with the ICC during a year-long investigation of match-fixing and betting.

October 28: CoA submits its tenth status report to the Supreme Court and marks out seven state-associations for failing to comply with the new constitution formed on the basis of the Lodha recommendations. They want the erring associations to furnish a compliance certificate within a set time-frame, failing which their voting rights would be suspended.

November 2: CoA wants the Supreme Court to reveal the names of the nine cricketers that the Justice Mudgal Committee had submitted to the apex court in a sealed envelope after investigating the 2013 spot-fixing scandal. The CoA made the request while replying to a public writ petition filed by Atul Kumar, a retired railway officer.

November 21: CoA-appointed three-member probe panel of Justice (retd) Rakesh Sharma, Barkha Singh, former chairperson of Delhi Commission of Women and lawyer-activist Veena Gowda clears Johri of sexual harassment allegations but recommends 'gender sensitivity counselling' for the top executive.

The verdict creates a rift in the two-member CoA, with Chairman Vinod Rai allowing Johri to resume his duties while the other member Diana Edulji remaining steadfast on her demand of seeking the CEO's resignation. Unnamed BCCI officials, according to media reports, back Edulji's stance, and press for Johri's resignation.

November 22: The exclusion of seasoned campaigner Mithali Raj from the World T20 semifinal against Australia creates a furore, as India lost the match by eight wickets. Fingers are pointed at captain Harmanpreet Singh and coach Ramesh Powar.

November 26: CoA member Diana Edulji says the committee will not interfere in Mithali's exclusion as it was a call taken by the team management. Her views contradicted those of CoA Chairman Vinod Rai, who had, a day earlier, indicated the committee will be meeting Harmanpreet, Powar, and Mithali.

November 27: Mithali's mail to BCCI CEO Johri and General Manager (Cricket Operations) Saba Karim is leaked to the media, a day after both the BCCI officials met Mithali and Harmanpreet.

November 29: Johri and Karim sumbit report on the Mithali-Powar spat to CoA.

December 7: BCCI acting-secretary Amitabh Choudhary questions CoA's functioning in a scathing letter to Karim.

PROLOGUE: THE MAN WITH A HEAVY BARITONE

26 March 2013

9:32 P.M.

An unidentified person from New Delhi dials a number in Pakistan. The call is then diverted to Dubai:

+9233332064488 (Pakistan): (No clear sound)

+971504560616 (New Delhi): *Salaam alaikum, bhai!*

+9233332064488: (No clear sound)

+971504560616: *Bhai, woh 7 million ka offer de raha hai woh apne ko.* (Bhai, he's offering us 7 million.)

+9233332064488: *Nahi, nahi, 7 mein toh nahi. Usko bolna ki 8 se kum nahi dena hai.* (Don't settle for less than 8.)

+971504560616: *Nahi, na? Aat se bilkul kum nahi . . .* (Yes, nothing less than eight.)

+9233332064488: *Haan, aat se kum nahi.* (Yes, nothing less than eight.)

+971504560616: *Theek hai.* (Okay.)

+9233332064488: *Mere khayaal se usne mujhe nau bola tha, lekin main bola tha aat. Apne aap malum chala tha aat se kam hum lenge hi nahi. Usne bol diya tha ki soch ke dho ya theen din mein jawab do. Apne ko malum hai ki saath ka hai apne paas.*

(He'd told me nine, but I said eight. Somehow, I felt we should not take less than eight. He had given us two or three days to think about the offer before reverting to him. I know we have another offer for seven.)

+971504560616: *Theek baat hai. Main aat bol ke chhod deta hoon.* (All right, I will leave it at eight.)

+9233332064488: *Aat bolke chhod do.* (Yes, leave it at eight.)

+971504560616: *Haan*! (Yes!)

+9233332064488: *Uska kya hua? Emirates Steel ka kuchh hua?* (And what about Emirates Steel?)

+971504560616: *Uska inshallah aaj ya kal ke andar kuchh hona chahiye. Abhi tak koi phone aaya nahi, lekin expected hai ki abhi, yeh karega contact abhi.* (They haven't called yet, but I am expecting they will contact me today or tomorrow.)

+9233332064488: *Woh atarah wala kya bolte, atarah wala?* (What happened to the deal of eighteen?)

+971504560616: *Woh aaya nahi kyon ki hum ne sadhe-unees apan ne bol diye tha na usko?* (He did not come back. We had asked for nineteen and a half, right?)

+9233332064488: *Haan, haan.* (Yes)

+971504560616: *Samjho, sadhe unees bol diye the phir usne phone hi nahi kiya aur apna dusra ek hai, samjhe? Inshallah hoga. Ek ya adha din mein kuchh na kuchh result ayega hi.* (If he doesn't agree for nineteen and a half, we have another one to go to. But some result is expected soon.)

+9233332064488: *Allah malik hai, accha.* (God will take care of everything.)

+971504560616: *Ek minute hai na? Chautani se baat karna.* (Bhai, please spare a minute and speak to Chautani.)

A new voice, Chautani, speaks: *Salaam alaikum,* hello?

+9233332064488: *Walekum salam, seth. Kya haal hai?* (*Seth,* how are you?)

+971504560616: Sir, *do carton le liya hai, aur Yemen mein jaunga to udhar honge to ek, do aur le lunga.* (Sir, I've picked up two cartons, and will pick up more when I go to Yemen, if available.)

+9233332064488: *Theek hai. Meherbaniya bahut, thank you.* (All right. Much appreciated. Thanks a lot.)

+9233332064488: *Pakki baat hai.* Hundred per cent (Certainly.)

+971504560616: Ok, sir. *Sir, apne minister saheb se pooch lijiyega.* (Sir, do ask the minister saheb.)

+9233332064488: *Minister saheb ke muh lagega toh teri ***** phat jayegi.* (If you confront the minister, you will be in trouble.)

+971504560616: *Accha, mooh lagne jaisa nahi hai?* (Oh, so it won't be worth confronting him?).

+9233332064488: *Mooh lagne jaisa nahi hai . . . raat ko teri baat kara deta hoon.* (Okay, so it's not confrontational, right? I will get him to talk to you at night.)[1]

●

In the quiet control room of the Delhi Police, where the call was being tapped, something about the tone and tenor of the voice from Pakistan rattled the listeners. There was an authoritative streak in that man's speech: he spoke slowly, mostly in monosyllables, but there was an unmistakable firmness in the voice that made them sit up and pay attention. Who was this man in Pakistan that big underworld names like Chautani were being deferential to? Could it be possible that this was *the* man himself? Somebody who commanded huge 'respect' among the fraternity. Their minds were racing. Could it be the don himself? Could it really be Dawood? The more rational and experienced minds said the voice couldn't be Dawood's, as he never spoke on a public telephone line. But maybe it was . . .

All these questions intrigued Delhi Police's Special Cell, which had been investigating the murky world of betting in cricket since 2012, after five first-class Indian players were caught in a sting operation talking about fixing; the outcome of a domestic match. The Special Cell's mandate was to identify active betting syndicates in India and their links with fixers and bookies. They also had a secondary agenda: to find out if the Board of Cricket Control in India (BCCI) could have possibly prevented the alleged malpractices in a game played solely under its watchful eyes.

The Special Cell had worked out a multi-pronged strategy to get the investigation underway. An incredibly high number of sleuths had been put on the job to gather all available details associated with the game, on and off the field. This meant gathering relevant, and sometimes a lot of irrelevant, information about current and former players, bookies and middlemen whose names had figured in various media reports. This also included details of their assets, associates, chosen medium of transactions and so on. The most important part of this investigation was to analyze, with the help of customized software, more than a thousand transcripts of conversations.

So far, most of the calls tracked by the Special Cell were about bookies, traders and some random calls about women. Long conversations about business, markets, trends, imports, exports, etc. had bored the listeners. The process had been grueling and tiresome, often with months of nothing even remotely usable coming their way. '*Kuch dhamaka chahiye, sir – lallu panjoo suntey suntey kaan pak gaye.* (We need something powerful. We're tired of listening to all this nonsense)' was the officers' refrain months into the arduous investigation.

Their wishes would be granted sooner than expected.

The months-long investigation had led them to stumble upon crucial information that suggested the world of betting and match-fixing went beyond their current ken, leaving room for an unpredictable conclusion. The investigators were beginning to fear there was a bigger and much more sinister connection in this whole set-up that would change the nature of the case: the underworld connection.

By February 2013[2], these doubts had become stronger, and they could begin lawful surveillance on the suspected international numbers. Phone conversations between Pakistan and Dubai were of particular interest to them. Due to the complex nature of international telecommunications and elaborate evasion techniques, these calls did not pass through any Indian gateways unless there was a systemic rerouting to bypass traffic congestion. The investigators had managed to intercept these calls and were tracking them on a continuous basis. They knew that this system of conferencing from one international terminus to another international conference station was the preferred mode of communication between international criminal syndicates.

The tracked global numbers along with those that were being dialed to India were getting connected to Delhi initially, which had thrown up an entire new set of phone numbers that needed to be put on surveillance. The police, armed with the home minister's permission, was prepared to begin the interception and recording of these phone calls, setting up the game for an interesting inning.

As the interceptions began, the officers held their breath: the network was far bigger and more intricately linked than they had imagined. It was turning out to be a full-fledged communications and operations network with bookies saddled in the country's capital, and connected to their partners in central and southern India while branching out to Nagpur, Thiruvananthapuram and Mumbai simultaneously. As they traced the betting hierarchy towards the very top of the pyramid, they found an exclusive group of people with a privileged access card of direct communication with the underworld bigwigs in Pakistan. The Special Cell had suspected that the biggest and most-dreaded name of them all was probably involved as well.

And then came this voice intercept.

The back office was abuzz with whispers: '*Yeh Bhai kaun hai? Regular nahi hai! Kya karey?* (Who's this guy? He is not a regular! What do we do now?)' Too many questions intrigued the investigators who had stumbled upon a fresh character in the trail of calls that had begun to feature people they could instantly identify based on voice patterns. This new voice was speaking easily of big money transactions – 7–8 crores – had to belong to someone in power. This figure intrigued the listeners. Was it millions in Indian Rupees or US Dollars? All they knew was that it had to represent a large sum, since even the negotiation to arrive at a figure between 7 and 8 was making a significant difference to both parties.

Other tip-offs in the call furthered the agitation: the typical Mumbaiyya slang, the Dongri mannerisms, the greetings in Urdu, the call routings, the *bhai–shagird* configuration, the ominous references to cartons (were they drugs, or weapons?), and the discussions about a co-conspirator at the level of a minister! Slowly, as the listeners took off their headphones and looked at each other, all of their faces reflected the same question: Had they just heard the voice of Dawood Ibrahim?

●

Betting in cricket has been part of public knowledge since the '90s. The police in India has always known about its existence, and there have been occasional raids and arrests that have not occupied more than a single-column space in the daily newspapers. However, it was only in 2000 that betting made it to the headlines, when it ended the careers of former Indian captain Mohammad Azharuddin and batsman Ajay Jadeja. 'Match-fixing' also spoilt the reputations of all-rounder Manoj Prabhakar and former Indian skipper and 'Haryana Hurricane' Kapil Dev, under whose captaincy India won its first cricket world cup. Though Kapil had wept on national television claiming innocence, it was too late. His name was forever linked to this dark world.

Since then, there had been whispers, but never any concrete evidence that match-fixing had once again earnestly commenced in the game. However, a sting operation by a media house during the 2012 Indian Premier League (IPL) exposed some first-class cricketers,[3] and alerted the police to the probability of things getting serious once again. As the investigation rolled on, members of the Special Cell began to understand that not only had fixing resumed in the game, but it had also taken on a new and better-organized avatar: it was now meticulously planned, entirely professional and well-executed. This match-fixing racket threatened to turn the cricketing world upside down.

Even before suspecting the Dawood connection, the Special Cell knew that there were a few Delhi-based conduits, unidentified until then, who were working in tandem with underworld bosses to successfully carry out the very profitable business of betting. These conduits were not merely taking bets on ongoing or forthcoming matches, but they were directly contacting cricketers to stage-manage certain matches for mutual windfall for all involved. This gambling machinery was facilitated by an unascertainable number of bookies.

The Special Cell had painstakingly devoted the past year to maintain recorded details of various calls between known entities, authenticate the codes used during these conversation as hints, trace any new numbers and more importantly, with the help of all possible resources – both on and off the field – spent hours listening to these callers and attempted to identify or locate the members to estimate the actual spread of this fiercely dangerous nexus. To expedite the process as well as ensure absolute confidentiality, the investigators had spread themselves to the suspected locations all over the country as civilians to gather information about those calling the shots, but until that day, 26 March 2013, they had not been able to get any evidence about who headed the entire proceedings.

Now, as news of the latest call spread, there was newfound energy and purpose in the control room. The team felt validated: all the deep digging of the previous year had led them to a veritable treasure chest, which had the potential to open up an even more challenging adventure. Suddenly, every single detail they had acquired, every conversation they had recorded, the calls they had listened to for countless hours, took on a new perspective.

The next step was to alert their boss, Delhi Police Commissioner Neeraj Kumar (IPS, 1976 Batch). Being a former officer with the Central Bureau of Investigation (CBI), he had his own network of various sources connected to the underworld. Neeraj Kumar had been privy to exclusive classified and unclassified information throughout his career, and, having interrogated several of the infamous underworld bosses himself, he had gained enough insight into this world. As a result of his experience, he had the ability to identify a caller merely by the manner in which he spoke and the language he used.

The moment the recordings were played to him, Neeraj Kumar realized the voice belonged to someone he had never heard before. That fact alone affirmed his worst fears. But for now, his first task was to get corroboration from the Research and Analysis Wing (R&AW).

The R&AW is India's primary external intelligence agency, organized on the lines of the American Central Intelligence Agency, and their main function is to collect external intelligence and counter-terrorism information via espionage, psychological warfare, subversion, sabotage and assassinations[4]. It maintains active collaborations with other secret services from various countries: FSB of Russia; NDS, the Afghan agency; Israel's Mossad; the CIA and MI6. All of them have a common interest: Pakistan's nuclear programme.[5]

Neeraj Kumar knew that R&AW would be the only Indian agency who could confirm the voice sample, after which it would have to be verified by the Central Forensic Science Laboratory (CFSL). This conversation could be the first direct telephonic conversation, never before a conversation had been been tapped before, establishing the involvement of Dawood Ibrahim in crime syndicates operating in India. So far, investigating agencies only had voice transcripts of Dawood's syndicate members like Chhota Shakeel and others, thus forcing them to book Dawood only as a conspirator. But this call could change that for good.

Neeraj Kumar desperately needed this case solved to redeem himself after the backlash he had faced in the Nirbhaya gang-rape case that had rocked the whole nation. The Delhi Police Commissioner found himself in the eye of the storm in that unfortunate case, and had almost resigned to accept an abrupt end to his illustrious career. However, this phone call could be his opportunity at redemption, and he was battle-ready this time.

It would not, of course, be easy. He was well aware that if his suspicions proved to be correct, and he informed various public sources, even a minor slip from his side would make him an easy target. Also, there was a powerful lobby consisting of various managers and senior members of the cricketing and political world, along with celebrities and businessmen, riding on the colossal equity of the IPL wave, who would not, by any means, appreciate this news. He had already faced the wrath of the NDA government under Vajpayee during his tenure as DGP with the CBI in 2000, when Kumar had alleged he had been forced to stop further investigations after the Hansie Cronje scandal.[6] That frustrating experience with the government was still fresh in his memory.

However, he knew it would be a rougher ride this time around. Earlier, it was only about naming a few cricketers involved in the fixing chain with close links to political bosses in the cricketing administration. This time, he was about to make public a name that would permanently taint the entire IPL bandwagon and attract immense negative international attention. For a league that was only just getting off the ground and acquiring momentum, this would be the worst possible outcome. If the Special Cell's suspicions turned out to be right, cricket, India's foremost passion, would become just another revenue stream of the underworld, and run by one of the most powerful gangsters and terrorists of all time.

Deciding to cross the bridge when he reached it, Kumar rushed into the night to set the wheels in motion. He had already alerted his colleagues in R&AW about the voice samples being dispatched to them for confirmation. R&AW had reassured him they would deal with the samples on a priority basis. By the time he arrived at the police headquarters, the report was already in. The R&AW officers had matched the samples to those they had collected from various global investigators, and unanimously declared their verdict: the voice belonged to none other than Dawood Ibrahim.

PART I

IPL AND THE D-COMPANY

1

THE D-CONNECTION AND CRICKET

Once it was confirmed that the unknown voice belonged to Dawood Ibrahim himself, the Special Cell members found themselves at sea. The scope of the investigation had just become much bigger than they'd imagined. They knew of Dawood – who didn't? But now they had to learn everything about him as a formal suspect; they had to understand his business empire and where cricket was placed in it. The time had arrived for a crash course in the world's most famous terrorist after Osama bin Laden.

The son of a police head constable, Dawood Ibrahim, a Konkani Muslim, was born Sheikh Dawood Ibrahim Kaskar on 26 December 1955. He laid the foundations of his notorious D-Company while behind bars in 1975.[1] He grew up as an amateur cricketer, first trying his hands at gully cricket, and in later years, watching every ball of every important cricket match from the best box at the pavilion end. Even as cricket remained his passion, his eye was set on the blind alleys of crime in downtown Mumbai.

Straying from his father Ibrahim Kaskar's wishes to follow his footsteps into the police, Dawood became a challenger to the Pathan gang. The Pathan gang was a term coined by the media in those days to describe organized criminal groups in Mumbai consisting of ethnic Pashtuns, largely immigrants from Afghanistan. They traced their origins to the 1940s, when a wave of Afghan immigrants came to Mumbai. From the growing Afghan community, crime lords such as Karim Lala emerged, running gambling and liquor dens out of which they operated their other illegal businesses. Starting out as a threat to the Pathan 'legacy', then becoming its leader, Dawood, along with Amirzada Pathan and his brother Alamzeb, built an organization that made him one of the world's richest yet least recognized organized-crime figures. Dawood had proved his prowess from being a daylight robber to becoming a successful smuggler. He had mastered the art of taking high risks in the most rewarding 'business of the hour' and managed his clients well. However, his relationship with the Pathan brothers was not to last very long.

Three years after his benefactors killed his eldest brother Sabir, Dawood exacted his carefully plotted revenge and cemented his grip over Mumbai's criminal world with the help of top-notch organizers, Chhota Shakeel, aka Shakeel Ahmad Babu, and Rajendra Nikhalje, aka Chhota Rajan. But in the wake of Sabir's murder, Dawood was forced to relocate his headquarters from Mumbai to Dubai.

Over the next nine years, the D-Company dabbled in land extortion, drug and weapons smuggling, and practically every other illegal endeavour imaginable, which were made easier by their rock-solid contacts across high levels in the government. Dawood's interests soon led him to Bollywood, where he became a major film financier.[2] In the 1980s, one would witness the crème de la crème of the film fraternity at his lavish parties. 'They wouldn't dare refuse an invitation,' said a friend of Dawood's, who preferred to remain anonymous.[3] He stated that those who opted out of these parties citing schedules would suddenly find their confirmed shooting dates cancelled or postponed, but no one could do anything about it. Nobody dared to upset the don.

Everything changed with the demolition of the Babri Masjid. The ensuing 1993 Mumbai blasts, the communal riots, all triggered by the underworld warlords, caused the Dawood gang to splinter. One of his top lieutenants, Chhota Rajan, often described by Dawood as one of his *nauratans* (nine jewels), defected and formed his own group consisting predominantly of Hindu boys. Dawood was accused of being the principal mastermind behind the blasts, ensuring he would never be able to return to India. He could not remain in Dubai either because of an Interpol alert for his arrest, along with the fact that UAE and India have an extradition treaty. Thus, Dawood fled to Pakistan, also moving his large family, comprising his wife, four daughters and a son, and certain close associates and their families out of Mumbai. One daughter, then aged twelve, subsequently died of malaria, and is said to have been buried in Pakistan.

As the Special Cell read the case files, they were amazed to discover the lavish lifestyle of one of the world's most wanted terrorists. Dawood was living like a king in Pakistan. His home was a palatial mansion spread over 6,000 square yards, and boasted a pool, a tennis court, a snooker room, and a private gym. He wore the best designer clothes, drove the most exclusive line of Mercedes and other such luxurious four-wheel drives, sported Patek Philipe wristwatches worth over half a million rupees, and showered money on starlets and prostitutes – virgins being his preference.[4]

According to reports, Dawood wakes up in the afternoon, and has his breakfast after a swim and shower. In the late afternoon, he gives his employees an audience where he briefs them on their assignments and they give him daily reports on his myriad businesses. If in the mood, he engages in a game of cricket or snooker with friends. As the sun sets, Dawood and his party set off for any one of his 'safe houses' in Karachi for an evening of revelry – usually comprising alcohol (Black Label is his preference), *mujras* and gambling. Carousing through the night, Dawood and his companions quit only at dawn and collectively offer fajr prayers. This daily routine and lifestyle became public when Pakistani investigative journalist Ghulam Hasnain wrote about it. Shortly after, he was abducted by the Pakistani Inter-Services Intelligence (ISI) and was reportedly tortured and then released with a warning to refrain from such subjects.[5]

But what perhaps galled the Indian police the most was to read about the fact that a number of Pakistani government undercover agents, who came in contact with Dawood because of their official duties, were now working for him. 'A major serves him a glass of water. Nearly all the men who surround him for security reasons are either retired or serving officers,' claimed an MQM activist.[6] 'And he keeps them happy – buying them expensive apartments, and showering them with favours. So they are more loyal to Dawood than to the Government of Pakistan.'

Not only have Pakistani authorities turned a blind eye to the activities of these gangs within Pakistan, but they have also partaken of Dawood's hospitality. Dawood often throws lavish *mujras* for Pakistani politicians and bureaucrats; it is alleged[7] that a former caretaker of the prime minister was his recent guest. It's not just the members of the establishment who have close ties with Dawood; he is also said to have the protection of assorted intelligence agencies. In fact, Dawood and his brother Anees have been provided round-the-clock armed security by the ISI. Besides, Rangers (paramilitary) from the Pakistani Army provide him with escorts during his movement within Karachi. His fleet has approximately six to eight land cruisers, most fitted with bulletproof glasses. The lane leading to his bungalow in Clifton in Karachi is barricaded and a police picket is at duty there.

Why would a nation as fragile as Pakistan put itself at risk by sheltering Dawood? wondered the Special Cell investigators. The answer turned out to be simple: Dawood was now Pakistan's number-one espionage operative. His men in Mumbai help him get whatever information he needs for Pakistan. Rumour has it that his men in Karachi sometimes accompany Pakistani intelligence agents to the airports to scan arriving passengers and identify R&AW agents.

As the investigators read on, they began to understand who they were up against. This wasn't a simple spot-fixing racket run by amateurs if it was being handled by someone as powerful as Dawood.

Ironically, despite arrests in India, his most famous and probably the only clear picture of him, which has him wearing a yellow T-shirt and sporting large, black sunglasses, was taken at the Sharjah Cup in 1987. Cricket was the one sport that Dawood was most passionate about, but that didn't stop him from using it to make money. In 1987, Dawood apparently even entered the dressing room of the Indian cricket team and tried inducing them to win.[8] Only they didn't know it was him! As Dilip Vengsarkar later revealed, 'Actor Mehmood was in our dressing room. Captain Kapil Dev had gone out to address the press. Mehmood introduced us to a big businessman from Sharjah. On his behalf, Mehmood said, "If you guys beat Pakistan tomorrow, everyone will get a Toyota car."'[9]

Vengsarkar went on to reveal that Kapil Dev had in fact asked Dawood to get out of the dressing room! Kapil confirmed the incident saying that he had asked the man to move out since visitors were not allowed inside the dressing room, and also because the team was due to have an informal strategy meeting. Apparently, he went away without rendering any response. It was much later that someone revealed his identity: a smuggler from Mumbai, known as Dawood Ibrahim. When the captain snubbed Dawood, Mehmood too, had to walk away along with him.

This incident also finds a mention in former BCCI secretary, the late Jaywant Lele's book, *I Was There: Memoirs of a Cricket*

Administrator. Lele, who claimed he did not know it was Dawood, writes: 'I and tour manager Dnyaneshwar Agashe went out of the room to meet this wealthy industrialist from Sharjah who promised to gift a Toyota car to each team member, including officials, at their doorsteps in India if they won. As bad luck would have it, India lost the tournament. Australia was declared champion on the basis of a higher run rate, as Australia, England and India earned equal points! After the results were declared most team members were not in tears, but that man was!'

Strangely, in terms of history, this was the second final against Pakistan that India lost. Exactly a year ago, history and Indian cricket fans would never forget the closest-ever final, where the final ball, which was hit for a six by Javed Miandad off Chetan Sharma, helped Pakistan win the trophy. Years later, Javed Miandad would become part of Dawood Ibrahim's family, when his son Junaid married Dawood's daughter Mahrukh in 2005.

Dawood's influence on the Pakistan cricket team has been an open secret for over a decade now. His name has also cropped up in scandals in neighbouring countries, including Bangladesh and Sri Lanka. According to Pakistani magazine *Newsline*, 'some of the Pakistani cricket players admit that at one time or another, they have sought Dawood's help, financially or otherwise.' Miandad's stint in cricket as a player and subsequently as a coach and administrator, despite opposition from other players, was reportedly at Dawood's behest.[10] Then in November 2011, a frightened and confused young Pakistani bowler called Mohammad Amir claimed he had been trapped by the underworld.[11] The day after Mohammad Amir pleaded guilty for the first time to charges of spot-fixing, a member of his family was approached in a Lahore mosque. The message was simple: Tell Amir to watch his step and watch what he says. Wasim Akram, incidentally the man who had hand-picked Amir in 2007, had also faced a similar incident. He claimed that his father had been kidnapped after his team lost a Test match against South Africa from a winning position in 1997.

Other events also pointed to the presence of Dawood in the sport. During the 1999 World Cup, *Dawn* newspaper's sports editor, Rishad Mehmood, had been summoned to an inquiry[12]. He was asked to explain how his newspaper had in a report predicted – more than 20 days before the match – that Pakistan, a top contender to win the tournament, might lose to minnows Bangladesh. Pakistan actually did lose to Bangladesh, who were subsequently awarded Test status by the International Cricket Council (ICC). Mehmood, unwilling to share details, alleged that the decision to lose, and many other decisions, were taken at a meeting involving a number of senior players in the World Cup squad weeks ahead of the tournament to draw up the team's strategy. 'All junior players at the time – such as Shoaib Akhtar and Shahid Afridi – were sitting outside, sulking, while the representative of a known underworld don Dawood were inside in the meeting.'[13] This is the same match that Ali Bacher, Chief of the United Cricket Board of South Africa (UCBSA), would bring up in April 2000 to deflect attention from the Hansie Cronje crisis that had racked South African cricket.

Around the same time as the 1999 World Cup, the body of a well-known Pakistani bookmaker, Hanif Kodvavi, alias Hanif Cadbury, was found badly mutilated in Johannesburg.

The speculation was that he had been killed for not returning the betting money.[14] Even in Bangladesh, cricketer Mohammed Ashraful, who admitted to spot-fixing and who was paid $ 12,800 to lose a match between Dhaka Gladiators and Chittagong Kings, confirmed that 'fixing' involved figures from the underworld. He has given information to the ICC Anti-Corruption and Security Unit, which is expected to help in unravelling the 'fixing' structure.[15]

On the whole, Dawood's entry into the fixing game was fairly easy to understand. The appeal of this additional revenue stream would be pretty obvious even to the average gangster. They did not have to *tapkao* anybody by way of some contractual killing. No land-grabbing was involved. No slum had to be forcibly evacuated. No tenant had to be threatened to make way for some developer. As an underworld ringleader put it, match-fixing was a 'clean job'. They only had to 'fix' a few players here and there and share the money. That was all. In the black world of crime, match-fixing had come to be known as 'white-collar business'.

As the police went through the cricket dossiers, they came across the Sharad Shetty era, which ended in 2003, when cricketers would regularly wine-and-dine with mafia lords and the seeds of match-fixing were first sown in the official records of law enforcers. By 2010, the windfalls from this cricketing business had reached a critical mass. It had prompted the Indian Intelligence Bureau (IB) to issue an alert[16] that funding for terror was drying up and the only two options available for the underworld to fund terror were *hawala* and cricket. The IB also claimed that the underworld did not invest money in the game directly, but looked to invest in it through its stooges. The operation was made to look legitimate in nature and would be a great challenge to track.

The much-glamourized IPL, in retrospect, was perhaps the perfect stage to set up a multi-crore 'enterprize' of such a nature. Not only were there ample opportunities and staggering amounts of money to be made, but the result of a match played between a glamorous mix of players from countries around the world made it look like a confirmed jackpot win on a free lottery ticket for the underworld.

As the Special Cell reached the end of the Dawood files, they couldn't help but hope for poetic justice: that maybe one day, the sport that he loved most in the world would be the route to extradite him back to India.

2

THE BIG BAD WORLD OF ILLEGAL BETTING

Betting on cricket matches had always existed in drawing rooms as well as *galis* and *nukkads*, mostly among friends and close acquaintances, much before the advent of highly professional betting exchanges. Ironically though, syndicated betting began on a major scale only after India won the 1983 World Cup, when the live telecast of matches featuring India, both at home and abroad, began on a regular basis. Soon after, betting started getting more organized and networked. Mumbai, India's financial capital and home to the Bombay Stock Exchange and the Mahalakshmi Racecourse emerged as the biggest centre for betting, followed by Delhi, Kolkata and Chennai. By early 1990s, besides the four metros, betting on cricket had spread to tier-two cities such as Ahmedabad, Chandigarh, Jaipur, Kanpur, Ahmedabad, Nagpur, Kochi and Hyderabad. But no matter how far it spread, it was the Mumbai bookies that opened the odds for any match being played anywhere. Even during the IPL scandal, although Ashwani Aggarwal alias Tinku Mandi, was a Delhi-based bookie-cum-fixer, Mumbai bookies retained their infamous claim to this position.

Interestingly enough, the first folks to ride the betting wave in cricket were bookies from the racing fraternity. This is why the person who places bets with a bookie in cricket is also termed a punter. And punters didn't need any particular reason to start betting. It just had to be a match that was being telecast live. Instead of horses, they had to only decide and speculate on the '*lambi race ka ghoda*' (a player who is expected to give his best) in a given match, and earn millions. Besides, unlike the limited popularity of horse racing, cricket was hugely popular with almost a fanatical fan following in India. Betting on cricket thus gave more returns than other sporting activities.

By the mid-1990s, with ODIs being telecast live, matches were brought home to even the farthest of corners of India. After cable TV, the next thing to change the face betting was the mobile phone. When mobile phones arrived in the 1990s, they came as a blessing for the bookies, who were no longer confined or dependent on government-owned static telephone lines. The mobile bookie was born. Even the internet played its part. With Internet access in India expanding twenty-fold in the mid-1990s to reach over 100 million people, the country, with its growing middle class and high appetite for betting, quickly became one of the most attractive markets for online gambling companies.

There are many different markets for cricket betting, and most of them depend on the nature of the match. But whether it's Ashes, T20 Internationals or One Day tournaments, there is always something for everybody: outright betting, match betting, betting on most sixes, betting on the top batsman, special bets . . . the list is expansive.

Whether it's international, domestic or even a series involving veterans, any betting activity is accompanied by the incessant clamour of ringing phones. If someone has access to live scores, all they need is a phone to become a bookie. Their operations become known through word of mouth. The notebook is the other key tool of trade. Every single activity of a bookie's professional life gets recorded in it – whether recommendations, instructions, or payments. This was evident in the case of bookie Ramesh Vyas.[1] If a punter wants to place his bets on a particular match, all that he needs to do is to make a call to his bookie, find out the odds and then place his bets for a particular amount. No money changes hands at this point of time and the punter's bet is duly entered by the bookie in his notebook in minimal and sometimes difficult-to-decipher language. It's only once the match is concluded that the exchange of money takes place and the notebook is destroyed.

In the early years, betting was mainly confined to the final outcome of a match, but over a period of time, betting on other aspects like the toss, individual scores and team scores – generally called 'spread betting' – also took shape. Another popular category of cricket betting is the 'total betting' markets. As the term indicates, the punter bets on just how many runs, fours or sixes, or a whole array of different things will happen in a match.

The most basic and popular form of betting would be to bet on the outcome of a match. Let's say you want to bet on a test series between India and South Africa. The different bets would be: India +$ 100, Tie +$ 210, South Africa +$ 275. If you bet on India to win, you will win $ 100 for each $ 100 you bet. If you think South Africa will win, you will win $ 275 for each $ 100 you bet. And if you wager on a tie, it will give you a return of $ 210 if you win. The objective in this is to predict which of the two teams will prevail in an individual match. The odds are weighed so that the payment for a winning favourite will be at less than even money, while a winning underdog will pay greater than 1–1.

Then there are the specialized bets:

Tied Match, where punters bet on a tie, draw, or a no-result due to factors like bad weather, crowd disturbance or walkout.

Series Winner, where bets are placed on which team will win a particular cricket series that are held throughout the year. This is a good way for beginners to learn cricket betting.

Win Toss, where bets are placed on which team will win the toss in a given match.

Innings, where the wager is on which team will outscore the other in an innings.

Match Scores, a wager on the total number of runs a team will have scored by the end of a match. Instead of choosing a specific number of runs, such as 156, the bet is usually made on a range, such as 150–60 runs. Predicting match scores is not at all easy, so the odds tend to be quite attractive.

Over/Under Scores, where bets are placed on the number of runs, but specifically on the total score of both the teams combined. The challenge is to identify correctly whether the final total will be over or under a given benchmark. Payouts tend to be very close to even money, minus the bookmaker's commission.

Top Batsman, where the bet is on which batsman will score the most runs, whether in a whole series, a single match or by a batsman from just one side. Other related forms are 'Top Home Batsman', 'Top Away Batsman', 'Match Top Batsman' and 'Top Series Batsman'. Again, this is not an easy wager to win, so it pays attractive odds. However, many bettors who know a team's line-up prefer this option. Also, bets on any player not in the starting 11 are void, and bets on players who take the field but do not bat may be settled as a losing wager.

Top Bowler, where the bet is on the bowler who will take the highest number of wickets. Like in the case of 'Top Batsman', this bet can be made on the overall series, for a single match or for just one side in a match, with the odds adjusted accordingly.

Man of the Match, where the objective is to identify which player will be accorded this top honour at the conclusion of the match. This option is usually available only for major contests. A popular variation is Player of the Series.

Another bet is one in which one has to correctly predict the number of runs that will be scored in the first over. Because this could be any one of several different figures, there can be some very large odds on offer if one actually manages to predict the number of runs. This is a bit like Russian roulette, and can have many variants – one can hazard a guess on the name of the player who is going to hit the most sixes or fours, or the player who will take the first wicket, or who will effect the most run-outs, or the player who will bowl the first ball of the match.[2]

The betting procedure is a flexible system in which odds keep changing depending on how the match is progressing. The punter can end a session of betting and place fresh bets as per his discretion. Normally, anybody who wishes to gamble on these probabilities accesses the last mile of a betting chain (it could be a small shop or a person or a telephone booth or any small retail outlet) and pays or promises to pay money on a certain bet organized by the bookies, and the punters decide on the volume of the total bet. Like every industry, the betting industry too has its own rules and ways of working. The odds for a particular match are decided by bookies based on certain accepted criteria such as the relative strength of the two teams, previous record, the nature of the pitch, weather conditions, team composition, etc. For example, if two teams, A and B, are scheduled to play, and if A is perceived to be weaker than B, the odds may be 60 paise on B and 150 paise on A. After these odds have been decided upon, primarily by Mumbai bookies, they are transmitted telephonically to bookies in different parts of India, and the betting begins. Punters then place bets with bookies over the telephone. Now if a punter places a bet of Rs 1 lakh on team B winning the match, he will get Rs 60,000 if team B wins. On the other hand, if he places a bet on team A, and if team A wins, he will get a sum of Rs 1.5 lakhs. However, if he loses his bet, then he pays Rs 1 lakh, which he had placed as a bet with the bookie concerned.

Then there are the more complex bets, where instead of betting on the outcome, a bettor can go for 'spread betting,' when the 'Single Index' equation comes into play. What defines this index is that it is independent of all other scores and events. For example: say England is playing India in a Test match and a Hussain is quoted at scoring 85–90 runs in both innings combined. The final result (the make-up) of this index will be the runs he scores in both innings. So if a punter thinks Hussain is likely to score more than 90, he buys at 90 for Rs 1 lakh. Let's look at the two scenarios:

(1) Say Hussain scores 52 in the first innings and 78 in the second. His total (the 'make-up') is 78+52 = 130. So the result here is (130-90) x Rs 1 lakh – i.e., the bettor wins Rs 40 lakh.
(2) Say Hussain scores 37 in the first innings and 0 in the second. His total (the make-up) is 37. The result here is a loss, because he scored less than 90, and so the bettor has to pay Rs 53 lakh (90-37 x Rs 1 lakh).

What is important to note here is that in order to reap a windfall, bookies will often manipulate the odds to seldom incur huge losses. It is generally the punter who risks losing his money.

The odds, which keep fluctuating as the match progresses, are transmitted to the bookies throughout India. Earlier, this was done over landline, then pagers took over, and now it is either by way of mobile phones or through the 'Dibba System.'[3] The Dibba is a phone with a speaker facility. The person operating the

Dibba normally has a mini-exchange in which there are 10 to 12 incoming and around 100 outgoing lines. An operator is constantly receiving the prevailing odds from the big bookies, which in turn are constantly passed on to other bookies or punters through the outgoing lines from the Dibba. The outgoing lines are also used by bookies or punters throughout India for latest information on prevailing odds in Mumbai, and are live throughout the match.

In the early 1990s, it was the ubiquitous STD/PCO booth owners who acted as conduits in this communication network. Later on, it gave way to well-organized betting exchanges in flats, high-rise shops or even offices of builders, as was evident during the raids on residences of Tinku Mandi and other bookies.[4]

An Indian betting syndicate's operations resemble that of a cartel's, meaning there are no two groups of bookies who fix odds at widely differing rates. This, to a degree, ensures there is no cut-throat competition that harms the bookies' interest, and that any differences are sorted out between themselves.

As betting caught on and the volumes increased rapidly, bookies and the underworld began exploring other tricks of the trade to encash on the trend. The syndicate realized that they needed to manipulate the results, and in order to do so, they had to fix a few players who would willingly do it for them for payment.

This is where the spirit of the game is compromised.

3

THE OLD FOX, SHARAD SHETTY

To understand how illegal betting has evolved in the game, and the relationship of the underworld with the business of cricket, one must first understand the past. The one name that was vital to shaping the underworld's interactions with cricket as we know it today and built the foundations of an empire that would grow to resemble the many-headed monster, we are now familiar with, was Sharad Shetty.

What people usually forget about Dawood is that he remains an ace businessman. In India alone, Dawood is believed to run a Rs 10,000 crore-plus empire that includes illegal mining, fake currency, betting syndicates, arms smuggling, real estate, commodities market investments, and garment businesses in two-tier cities. While his passion for cricket is well-documented, it is first and foremost a profitable revenue stream, so it stands to reason that he would appoint one of his best men to run it.

Sharad 'Anna' Shetty and Dawood began a long and mutually prosperous relationship way back in 1979, when both worked as smugglers, and aided goons challenging the regime of the legendary crime lord Karim Lala. The Dawood–Anna pair utilized an air smuggling route known as the 'sweeper line' using the garbage dumps as pick-up and drop spots to transfer gold in and out of Mumbai airport and avoid the newly installed X-ray machines. The scheme made both men rich, but resulted in charges against both under the Conservation of Foreign Exchange and Prevention of Smuggling Activities Act (COFEPOSA) of 1974. Both were released soon after and maintained friendly relations.

While Dawood returned to smuggling, Shetty amassed a string of high-end hotels, bars and restaurants that he used as fronts for his illicit activities. Among his most impressive holdings were the Regent Palace and the Regal Hotel. He was the head of the Rami Group of Hotels, in addition to serving as the godfather of a large-scale bookie ring that specialized in match-fixing. Few could match the avarice with which Shetty pursued wealth and power; only his friend could be called his superior in this regard.

After Shetty began working with Dawood, he became the landing agent for the D-Company in the Madh–Marve region. During the late 1980s, when Chief Minister Sharad Pawar decided to de-reserve land in the western suburbs of the city, a frantic rush ensued, but the first to establish his sway over the turf was Shetty. He was already receiving huge amounts from builders as protection money, and this would only increase as they entered the booming construction market of the West. And it more than helped that Shetty had grown up in Jogeshwari.

But if the lure of land in Mumbai was strong enough to tear families apart, it also had drove a wedge in the criminal empire. When Dawood's most trusted hitman Rama Naik, who controlled the eastern side of Central Mumbai, staked his claim to a plot in Jogeshwari, a war of sorts broke out. Shetty refused to give in and the two men were at loggerheads. The Jogeshwari slums were cleared out in just twleve hours, but the gunmen of neither dons were willing to back down.

Finally, Dawood interceded, in typical godfather style, on behalf of Shetty, resulting in a vertical split in his empire. From thereon, the relationship strengthened. Even as Shetty won favour with Dawood, he roused the ire of other members with his steady climb. Rama Naik, especially, was sore at the loss of favour and land, but couldn't do much as he was murdered at Shetty's behest, in 1988.

As Shetty grew from strength to strength, it was only natural that he would be handed control of the cricketing business, given his background in illegal gambling. Dawood, along with Shetty, became the usual suspects at Sharjah matches for many years, from 1991[1] up until the 2003 World Cup.

Shetty proved himself adept at the new task. He quickly established himself as a kingpin. An intelligent man, Shetty could memorize phone numbers of cricketers and bookies across the globe. He kept track of every detail of cricket matches, beginning with the toss, incorporating the nuances of the game. He bribed, coaxed, cajoled and threatened cricketers from all over the world into following his script. Equipped with the flow of what was going to happen, he fixed the odds to favour the bookie and to suck the gullible punter into betting on what he had ensured would not happen. Moreover, the D-company's hundreds of proxy *hawala* and money-exchange outlets in Dubai's Deira and Naif areas provided quick currency transactions to any part of the subcontinent.

Until, Shetty came into the picture, betting and influencing the bets was mostly a small-scale, quick-cash business. It was Shetty who developed this into a full-fledged opportunity, generating huge cash and refuelling the *hawala* networks for all their allied businesses. Though most overseas deals were struck by bookies close to Shetty, he took it upon himself to place the odds when an India–Pakistan match was on. The approximate turnover for a match between the subcontinental rivals was close to Rs 250 crore and that's where he made most of his ill-gotten gains. In certain matches, Shetty was known to have ordered Indian bookies not to take bets, as wagers in Dubai were much higher.

Of course, it helped that he had charm too. His proximity to ex-Indian and Pakistani cricketers, some of whom were linked to the match-fixing scam, was well known. Shetty was even alleged to have parked the 'illegal monies' of some players and their relatives in his businesses, thus saving them embarrassing explanations and delivering a phenomenal return on investment at the same time. But he was most famous for his 'dinners', where he would create a pleasant atmosphere for cricketers and their 'fans' to indulge in extravagant evenings of food and wine, and make it seem almost natural to have an across-the-table conversation on the team composition or their opinion on the pitch and conditions, perceived changes in the batting order, batsman fitness levels, or who they thought would open the bowling – all innocent questions that fans pose to cricketers everywhere.

As the relationships with the cricketers evolved, Shetty began bringing 'small gifts' to cement them further, moving the relationship from beyond merely answering questions to volunteering information – anything that could give his bookies an edge. This 'friendship' was more insidious than any direct bribe or a threat. Cricketers would think, if a nice fellow like Shetty, a good friend, made some money off the game, where's the harm in that? For instance, Shetty was known to have cultivated a close relationship with Indian captain Mohammad Azharuddin and even gifted him a Rolex. During the course of the 2000 match-fixing investigations, the police stumbled upon many other cricketers who were close to Shetty.

But running the country's largest betting business with crooked bookies and cunning punters was not always a party. Shetty went on to be charged with murder and extortion in more than five cases. He fled the country for Dubai in 1990, where his hold on Indian cricket as well as his other businesses continued to flourish. He became the owner of two hotels there and had stakes in many restaurants, nightclubs and hotels in Abu Dhabi.

It is believed that Shetty came close to being trapped by the Indian police once. They had provided a lead to Interpol about his illegal activities in Dubai as well as his whereabouts, but the wily fox managed to stage his own arrest in a petty criminal case in the United Arab Emirates and thus managed to avoid extradition to India. He knew that under the terms of agreement, an accused could not be extradited unless the case reached its logical end in the UAE, which in any case was bound to take a few years. Thereafter, all efforts to extradite Shetty after his arrest in Dubai on 26 November 1997 proved futile.

The cricket and betting networks created by Shetty were so strong and interrelated that it took the cops years to even identify that it was at play. But this party was soon going to end, with Shetty's success striking a dagger in the heart of Dawood's arch rival – Chhota Rajan.

Once the most trusted aide of Dawood, Chhota Rajan turned into his deadliest enemy after the split. Rajan ran his cartel from chartered ships and yachts on the high seas via satellite phone. Said to be close to Indian intelligence agencies, Rajan developed himself into Dawood's counterpart at every level and now his sights were on Shetty.

Despite his criminal sophistication, Shetty was also a notorious snitch. During September 2000, Shetty was known to have played a role in the near-fatal ambushing of Chhota Rajan, an attack that claimed the life of Rajan's underboss, Rohit Verma. Once Rajan learnt that Shetty had taken part in the plot against his life, he initiated a retaliatory plan, which was two years in the making.

On the night of 19 January 2003, four gunmen pumped 20 bullets into the body of Shetty, as he sat in Karma, the popular bar at one of the most elite clubs in Dubai, India Club. The location was the hangout for Dawood's henchman, Muthappa Rai, yet another victim of Shetty's loose tongue. Shetty was the victim of a conspiracy orchestrated by Chhota Rajan, carried out with the help of Rai. The shooting was revenge for both men and allowed Rai to exercise greater autonomy in his territory.

This was, however, not the only theory behind Shetty's killing. After his death, the IB floated a new theory. According to them, 'Of late, Shetty was growing in stature, and Anees, who enjoyed the second-in-command status in the D-gang, was getting insecure. There's a possibility that the D-gang itself turned against him.'[2] Intelligence officials cite the instance of the arrest of Dawood's brother, Anees, in Dubai a few weeks before Shetty's death as proof. Shetty may have tipped off Dubai authorities about Anees travelling on fake documents. They had to pick him up but Anees was surreptitiously let off and then transported to Karachi. The conspiracy theory, however, was put to rest, as Chhota Rajan announced his intention to take over the betting syndicate by claiming credit for Shetty's killing. Four of Rajan's gang members – Karan Singh Mansingh, Manoj Mudanna Kotian, Amar Bahadur Bam and Vimal Kumar Ram – were later arrested, tried and executed in the UAE for the crime.

The loss of Shetty would prove to be big for the D-Company. He had not only been their gambling specialist, but he was also the one with the contacts, the reputation and the personality. The group had to find a suitable replacement immediately, or risk losing ground to Rajan and his allies. But the D-gang floundered and Rajan managed to take over a lion's share of Dawood's cricketing business, offering bookies, instead of Shetty's brand of friendship, the valuable muscle-power that could help them recover cash in a business where people often went back on their word.

The death of Shetty in 2003 signalled the end of the bookie–fixer combination and launched an era of the super-punter. Shetty had a knack to pull off two mutually contradictory requirements: while on one hand, he rubbed shoulders with top cricket stars who lived their lives in the harsh glare of the spotlight, on the other, he remained a will-o'-the-wisp, invisible to authority. That combination of being a fixer and bookie both earned him the title of 'super-punter'. He had prepared the bookie network at the 2003 World Cup and some believe even decided the fate of a few matches. As destiny would have it, the World Cup began twenty days after he was shot dead.

The ironic part of Shetty's legacy is that even though he played for the other side, he did a phenomenal job. So much that, even today, cops investigating bookie–punter networks rely on Shetty's dossier and some close punters who had worked with him. There was only one Sharad Shetty, and the instability of the cricketing business of the D-Company for many years after his death would stand testimony to that.

•

In the years following Shetty's death, there was a vacuum in the D-Company on the cricketing-business front. Who could take Shetty's place and handle fixing and betting with the same ease and expertize? According to intelligence reports, Anees Ibrahim and Chhota Shakeel had been overseeing this portfolio, but it wasn't the core business for either of them, as they had their own portfolios to handle. Anees was the frontman for all of Dawood's businesses. The pressure by Indian agencies had virtually forced Dawood to go underground, leaving the charge to his younger brother. Anees worked as the classic frontman for Dawood, operating from a spacious office at Pearl Building in Deira, Dubai, taking telephonic orders for consignments and fixing deals, all with the tacit nod of Dawood in Karachi.

The face of D-Company's crime syndicate, Shakeel, lived in Karachi's posh defence area and ran the terror–extortion racket. He directly reported to Dawood and handled the gang's network across India, Nepal, Bangladesh and Thailand. The authorities soon learnt that Dawood had placed Shakeel in charge of his Mumbai operations, including betting syndicates. Shakeel mastered the art of intimidation, personally calling his victims to issue threats and make extortion demands. In spite of his small stature, a mere 5'2", Shakeel's voice became an effective and terrifying tool in raising funds. But he did not have the pedigree or the expertize to talk to bookies, players and punters, and scale the business. He was good only as a recovery agent.

Arif Bhaijaan, Chhota Shakeel's brother-in-law, came on board to help with the running of D-Company's betting and match-fixing operations, but he was arrested along with seven accomplices to not only break the gang, but also to obtain information on the D-Company lieutenant, Mohammed Dossa. Bhaijaan also faced charges in relation to the beating up of a Mumbai bookie who owed him money.

As the D-Company scrambled to get its cricketing business into shape between 2003 and 2012, there was a corresponding decrease in pressure from the government on Dawood himself.

For these eight-odd years, Dawood seemed to have gone under the radar of all intelligence agencies, and there were no bans, alerts or Interpol notices on him. One reason for this could be that the War on Terror had intensified and America was busy chasing Osama. Pakistan, they knew, would be an important ally if they ever had hopes of finding Osama, and maybe that was why the hunt for Dawood abated. Whatever the reason, the fact remains that the agencies didn't pay any real attention to Dawood for over a decade after he had been named a Specially Designated Global Terrorist in October 2003 and even a couple of years later, when his organization was called a Significant Foreign Narcotics Trafficker. The US dossier even mentioned Chhota Shakeel as Dawood's lieutenant who coordinated for the D-Company with other organized crime and terror groups, and Tiger Memon as a trusted lieutenant who controlled the group's businesses across South Asia.

It was only when the 2012 fixing scam came to light that Dawood and Tiger Memon once again came under the US radar.

After Osama's death, the US once again started targeting the 'nexus of crime and terrorism' in South Asia. It designated Dawood's two top aides as key drug traffickers, and slapped sanctions on them. Interpol also issued provisional arrest warrants or 'red notices' on Shakeel and Memon. As a result of this action, American citizens were prohibited from conducting financial or commercial transactions with Chhota Shakeel and Tiger Memon, and any assets they had under US jurisdiction were frozen.

This changed the game. Suddenly, the freedom of the D-gang to operate and run their various businesses worldwide was curbed;

hence, the only easy way out for generating quick cash for 'sundry' additional activities (like drugs, weapons and terror facilitation) was sports betting and fixing. This was corroborated by a senior officer from the IB (now an Interpol representative) who believed that due to the events of 2012, there was greater pressure on Dawood to earn money, and betting was the easiest business to fill that need. This is where experts suggest Dawood decided to run the cricket business himself, using Shakeel merely as an 'executor' instead of expecting him to fill Shetty's shoes. Shetty had run the business as his personal fiefdom, rarely involving Dawood, but now Dawood would be the strategist and use the aggressive Shakeel as his lieutenant.

This increased focus on cricket was, however, dismissed by Shakeel in an interview to *Times of India* that took place in the aftermath of the 2013 fixing scam, where he said their gang had left the cricket betting business altogether[3]:

TOI: Your gang's name has cropped up in the betting racket. Please explain.
Chhota Shakeel: Initially, our gang was involved in betting and match-fixing and it was entirely handed by Bhai's trusted man Sharad Anna (Sharad Shetty). Anna passed away in 2003 and since then we have been out of it. Bhai has strictly warned us to stay away from betting. We are into real estate now. Have you heard of us calling up anybody and threatening them in the last few years?
TOI: Earlier, your gang was involved in betting and *hawala* operations.

Shakeel: Yes, our gang was involved in the controversy involving Hansie Cronje but after that we are out of it. None of Bhai's family members, not even his brother Anees, is involved.

TOI: Do you know Sunil Abichandani, alias Sunil Dubai, who is being linked to you?

Shakeel: We know Sunil but that does not mean we are involved. Like him, there are several people we know who are associated with betting and match-fixing. That does not mean we are involved. We have grown now; we have left those days far behind. We are into real estate and other white businesses. Bhai does not want this *haram* money coming out of betting.

TOI: Then why is your gang's name getting linked with this?

Shakeel: We have been watching press conferences by the Mumbai and Delhi cops and reading newspapers on the Internet. Neither Delhi Police Chief Neeraj Kumar nor Mumbai Joint Commissioner Himanshu Roy has named us. There are some channels that are putting our gang's name into police officers' mouths. It's easy for the channels to do that as we do not get a chance to deny it. And news channels want our name so that their TRPs go up and they can show their stories make a big impact.

●

Chhota Shakeel was obviously talking nonsense. Not only was the D-Company active in betting circles, but Dawood himself had also recently lost a bet of Rs 50 crore. It's the kind of money that makes news, no matter how much you try to hush it up.

In the 2010 Pakistan versus England Test series, which would later come to be known more for the spot-fixing scandal that implicated three players of the Pakistan team than the cricket itself, bets of Rs 300 crore were riding on the fourth Test, and Rs 50 crore had been bet from Mumbai alone, sources said.[4] Pakistani bookie Mazhar Majeed was assigned the task of spot-fixing this match by fixing two no-balls in two overs, and not more. The information was made available to all the bookies who had links with Dawood's betting syndicate.

Everything happened as per the plan. Both Mohammad Amir and Mohammad Asif bowled one no-ball each and the bookies made huge profits. But the tables turned when Asif bowled a third no-ball. It left the bookies in Mumbai stunned as they incurred huge losses. This third no-ball cost Dawood Rs 50 crore in Mumbai alone.

Dawood's men in Mumbai – Junior Kolkata and Kothari – called up their boss, Sunil Dubai, after the third no-ball. They requested him to call off the bets, as following the third no-ball, Mumbai's bookies had started demanding they return their money. Sunil Dubai then informed Shoaib Khan, who ran Dawood's syndicate from Karachi. Shoaib made it clear that any hue and cry over the botched fixing could expose the syndicate, so it was better to return the money and bear the loss.

But personal loss notwithstanding, what emerged from the fallout was that Dawood was now playing a more active role in this business. He was not only deciding on betting rates for IPL matches personally, but he was also employing muscle power, warning people down the chain himself to cooperate, and bribing officials. He had not done this in years. A lot of cops and bookies believed Dawood was actively manipulating the odds on a likely winner through his bookies to exploit the last-minute deliberate dramas in a match, and turn them into large-scale bets. However, this also meant he was in direct contact with the bookies and thereby much more 'visible' in the business, as many police statements would later reveal. 'All match-fixers are answerable to Dawood Ibrahim,' claimed a top Pakistani bookie.[5]

In 2009, when South Africa pulled off a historic series win at the Melbourne Cricket Ground, several bookies who had betted on Ponting lost heavily. Just before the series, many had put their money on Australia beating South Africa. But the latter defied all odds to win the series, and the bookies had to cough up a lot of money. One of the D-Company punters defaulted on payments worth Rs 25 crore. Bookie Hitesh Samrat set his recovery agents into action. Only when Chhota Shakeel intervened did Samrat relent and agree to wait for the dues to be settled in the next betting season.

In May 2012, it came to light that the D-Company had succeeded in bribing high-ranking officers in the Mumbai Police. This 'fixing of cops' was Dawood's signature move since he belonged to the police stock, and knew its internal structures very well. This information had come from a bookie called Sonu Yogendra Jalan, alias Maladwas, who was busted in a police raid at Lokhandwala. It turned out that his network alone had a turnover of around Rs 500 crore a month, and was controlled by Chhota Shakeel. They had paid PKR 10 crore to a Sri Lankan cricketer for fixing a match. Sonu, while in custody, also told the police that he had paid around Rs 1 crore to a senior IPS officer to avoid an arrest, but in vain. When he threatened to lodge a complaint with the state anti-corruption bureau, it was believed that another police officer intervened and stopped the matter from getting out of control.[6]

The size of the bribe, the bribing of not one, but two high ranking officials, and the extent of Sonu's network tipped off the police that Dawood himself was pulling the strings. But they wondered at this sudden micromanagement of a hitherto outsourced function. The police could see no other reason other than the fact that this income stream had suddenly become critical to Dawood. The question remained – why? The answer, or what they suspected as the answer, came in a recorded call between Dawood and bookies where Tiger Memon was discussed. The timing of the call, which took place in the midst of IPL 2013, was itself a big clue:[7]

Dawood: *Salaam Waleikum!*

A: You stay a thousand miles away. Had to wait two days!

D: You know how it has been. Also, Saleem's wedding . . . By the way, you didn't come for the wedding.

A: Yes.

D: What a wedding it was! Ask me! Had many drinks. Slept throughout the day. Woke up at eight and then was at the treadmill for 15 minutes.

A: That work in Islamabad has been done. Ahmed has confirmed it's Memon's letter. But we couldn't get the letter. But the Chairman keeps asking about it.

D: Arshad has got the letter. I will read it out to you. A subordinate has confirmed the work is done.

A: Yes, but he [the Chairman] keeps asking for the letter every day.

While investigations into the context of this 'letter' continued, the police found this conversation significant for other reasons. Dawood had sounded pensive, almost nervous, for the first time. Secondly, it was also the first time the police had direct evidence that the dreaded Tiger Memon was still active and involved in various terror activities. It was obvious that the D-Company felt the need to protect him from any international pressure. And lastly, the timing of the call, followed as it was by a conversation with a bookie about monies, led the police to ask the question: was there any possibility that the money from cricket betting was being diverted into terrorist activities?

This angle had previously been investigated on at least three occasions: first, when the match-fixing scandal broke in India in 2000; second, during the expose by Tehelka on India TV in 2012; and third, during the Pakistani cricketers' involvement in the 2010 spot-fixing scandal. But nothing came to light and the terror angle could not be proved beyond a point.

Without the terror-funding angle, match-fixing continues to be a victimless crime, so the punishment for it never involved the real criminals – the underworld. But thanks to Neeraj Kumar, the underworld angle had finally been unearthed, and the charge sheet filed by the cops in the 2013 IPL fixing scandal furnished proof of their involvement. All this meant the angle could now be investigated vigorously and the powers-that-be could look at match-fixing with the seriousness it deserves.

4

THE GANG'S FAMILY TREE

It is needless to state that a crime of a magnitude such as illegal betting in cricket, involving such varied actors based across several locations abroad and in the country, cannot be committed unless there exists a meticulously planned criminal conspiracy having multiple interests with a common goal.

The roots of this conspiracy lie in the greed of the Dawood Ibrahim–Chhota Shakeel syndicate, which has over the last thirty years indulged in crimes of varying sophistication in pursuit of earning illegitimate wealth. There was a meeting of minds between the core syndicate members and their appendage – the fixers, the financiers, bookies, the *hawala* operators and the ultimate executors, i.e., the cricketers. Cops who stumbled upon the conversation involving Dawood could infer that a criminal conspiracy was in the making, waiting to be executed at opportune occasions.

The biggest influence the D-gang has had in the fixing–betting market has been in the integration of local Indian betting markets with their Pakistan- and Dubai-based counterparts. This integration of markets along with the streamlining of money transfers through *hawala* and the certainty of settlements by muscle power has opened up a huge avenue for windfall gains for this syndicate.

The 2013 IPL spot-fixing case, which rocked the nation, was an amalgamation of multiple sub-conspiracies, all controlled and directed by the mega conspiracy in which Dawood and Chhota Shakeel were the prime movers. The phone call intercepted by the Special Cell had involved Javed Chautani, a close associate of Dawood. Chautani was identified as part of the first layer – the initiators and authors – who were the overseas-based members of Dawood's syndicate. Each of these initiators ran a network headed by primary bookies. Since organized criminal syndicates operated on a strict need-to-know basis, the Dawood–Shakeel combine would never speak to any of their associates based in India over phone or any other medium that would be prone to legitimate interception by Indian law enforcement agencies. The core conspirators based in Pakistan believed they were safe and beyond interception by Indian law enforcement agencies. Chautani himself was not a suspected criminal and found no mention on the Indian 'Wanted' list, ensuring that any communication between him and an Indian entity would remain beyond suspicion and interception, and be treated as a routine affair, which justified the uninhibited communication between Chautani and his primary bookie.

But when the Special Cell followed the trail of Chautani's phone calls, they stumbled upon another name that kept appearing in the recordings: Tinku Mandi, a thirty-three-year-old man from Delhi's Adarsh Nagar. His real name was Ashwani Aggarwal.[1] He used to operate from the vegetable market and hence had acquired the moniker of Mandi. The cops were left in no doubt that Tinku Mandi was the principal Indian conduit, acting on behalf of his Pakistan bosses in order to execute the IPL spot-fixing racket and ran a full-fledged betting exchange from his rented flat in Gurugram. The flat was equipped with a 40-inch LCD TV aided by a TV decoder of Set Max as well as by assorted paraphernalia. Around this sat his associates, using six laptops, iPads, and various internet and international calling cards. The flat had installed Wi-Fi routers for seamless Internet connectivity.

IPL Season 6 was to begin from 3 April 2013. The investigators could see that the underworld network in Dubai and Pakistan had been communicating with Tinku since February 2013. As the investigation gained momentum and they delved deep into the work done by Tinku, they realized he was leading a nationwide network of fixers and bookies from India, and running a betting exchange using more than thirty-two telephone connections registered under fake identities or obtained by impersonation.

The police had linked Tinku with the underworld, and was privy to conversations that discussed the methods by which the underworld was executing the operations. So far, most of the incriminating evidence either pertained to foreign lands or did not promise to deliver much in terms of actually pinning down the culprits. The police needed actual physical evidence of the involvement of those who would be active partners in the crime: the players themselves.

At this stage of the investigation, there was only rampant speculation about how players were recruited and what made them agree. Why would a respected sportsman put his name and career on the line? Was it just for the money? The answers would emerge in time and would range from mistresses to blackmail, but sadly they would find that the situation rarely reached the final stage of confrontation or coercion – most wickets did fall right at the mention of the word 'money'.

On the question of recruitment, the picture was still blurred. There were many dots to be connected before the final picture could emerge. Logic demanded that players would not entertain these offers unless they came from a source they trusted. The phone trail so far showed no direct contact between players and known members of the underworld. Clearly, several layers were at play and the strands connecting the two parties were complex and interwoven. Thankfully, with the detection of Tinku Mandi, the police were finally able to begin the slow and painful process of unravelling this tightly wound-up ball of wool.

The phone interceptions and hours of tape continued to roll on Tinku Mandi, eventually leading them to two men in their early forties from Nagpur, Sunil Bhatia and Kiran Dhole. It would be Sunil Bhatia, resident of Nagpur's New Colony, who would eventually lead them to their first catch amongst the cricketers: Rajasthan Royals' bowler Ajit Chandila. Bhatia and Dhole were the fixers who had managed to hook Chandila. But after Bhatia's arrest and confession, a can of worms opened up.

According to Bhatia, he had come to Delhi in 2008 to attend a friend's daughter's wedding. There he had befriended one Rishi

Goyal, who asked him if he knew any cricket players. Bhatia knew Baburao Yadav, who was playing in the now-defunct Indian Cricket League (ICL), and he arranged for a meeting between Rishi and Baburao. The meeting, held in his presence, was about fixing match sessions. This is where Bhatia was roped into the racket. In 2011–12, he met Ashwani, alias Tinku Mandi, at a hotel in Nagpur through his friend Pappu Aggarwal, alias Mausaji. Tinku Mandi, he learned, was a well-reputed bookie-cum-fixer in Delhi. Meanwhile, Baburao Yadav had introduced Bhatia to Ajit Chandila, and so Bhatia introduced Chandila to Tinku. The wheels were set in motion.[2]

With Chandila's phone number now under constant interception, the police were able to trace more bookies, this time in Mumbai, an area that had been relatively untouched by the investigators so far. Chandila's contact person here was a guy in his mid-30s, known as Chandresh Patel or Chand Bhai to the betting world. He lived at Four Bungalows, Andheri.

But Tinku Mandi was not the only big bookie Chautani was managing. Just like Tinku, there were other prominent bookies, like Ramesh Vyas, Feroz, and Jitendra Jain alias Jeetu Tharad. The 'Ramesh Vyas Pyramid' involved Chandresh Jain alias Jupiter, Salman alias Master, while the 'Feroz Pyramid' had Master as the common contact and additionally a man called Ehteysham. The 'Jeetu Tharad Pyramid' had Chand Bhai, Manan Bhatt and others as its members.

The Vyas Pyramid, mentioned above, spread out to another overlapping set of conspirators, which had Tinku Mandi as its common node. New entrants like Sunil Bhatia, Kiran Dhole and

Ajit Chandila were found joining the grand plan. This branch and its connectivity and acquaintance with the core conspirators – Dawood Ibrahim, Chhota Shakeel and Javed Chautani – is cogently established by the confessional statement of Sunil Bhatia.

The pyramid[3] involving Feroz also had sub-branches, the first one with Vyas as a common node, and Jupiter and Master as members. The second sub-branch had Feroz as the common node, and again Salman, and Ehteysham and other Indian as well as Pakistani bookies, as its members. All of this was revealed in phone interceptions and legally admissible confessions.

The third branch originating from Javed Chautani had Jeetu Tharad as its common node. All these separate yet linked sub-conspiracies had fixers who were approaching players through either current players known to them or ex-players. Thus, fixers Sunil Bhatia and Kiran Dhole were approaching players through Manish Guddewar and Baburao Yadav, while fixers Jeetu Tharad, Chandresh Patel and Manan Bhatt were utilizing the services of Amit Kumar Singh. Between the different chains were a few bookies or local cricketers who would talk to members of other chains, oblivious to the fact that they were part of a larger chain.

Eventually, the fixers were all approaching the players, who were to be the executors of their nefarious plans in the stadium. In this network, Chandila was linked to both Chandresh Patel (whose bookie was Jitendra Jain) as well as to Sunil Bhatia (whose bookie was Tinku Mandi), apart from several others. Similarly, Rajasthan Royals bowler Ankeet Chavan, who was also arrested during the 2013 IPL spot-fixing scandal, was linked to both the aforementioned fixers, apparently belonging to different subsets of conspirators. Interrogation of the arrested – a former Vidarbha local player and the two fixers – revealed that cricketer Ajit Chandila was the key fixer in the 2013 scandal. Almost all the bookies had approached Chandila first, who then contacted other players and arranged for meetings. Chandila, the police said, was in touch with four sets of fixers. This meant he could have spot-fixed more than once in a match, with or without letting the other fixers know. It was easy for him to have fixed more number of matches by playing for different sets of people.

The police had a daunting task at hand, i.e., to try and ascertain if the four sets of fixers Chandila was in touch with had a common kingpin. Although there were a few more IPL players who were actively conniving with the fixers, the investigators were not sure if the players knew from the first day itself who among them was biting the bait, except for those whom Chandila had brought to the other side, where the rules were written by the fixers.

The cooperation of former players like Manish Guddewar, Amit Kumar Singh and Baburao Yadav, who facilitated the contacts of fixers/henchmen with current players, was essential to this scheme. The names of Guddewar and Baburao were all part of an interesting trend: one where former cricketers turned bookies and played key roles as conduits. Apart from the two Rajasthan Royal players – Chandila and Chavan – Indian Test bowler S. Sreesanth was also arrested; arrested bookies Jiju Janardhan and Amit Kumar, alias Amit Singh, had all played cricket league. While Jiju – also known as Sreesanth's 'satellite' – played for Ernakulam, Manish Guddewar was a former Vidarbha state player as well.

It would be the third branch, the 'Jeetu Tharad Pyramid', with the assistance of Manan Bhatt, a twenty-six-year-old from Ambavadi in Ahmedabad, who would ultimately deliver to the police their big fish, S. Sreesanth, a famed Test bowler who had made the headlines for his lively bowling and livid temper.

As the police waded through the conversations and past relationships to establish the links between the various branches of this immense family tree of fixers and betters, the police had no doubt that at the root of all these branches was the grandmaster himself: Dawood Ibrahim. But was the don orchestrating the whole network himself? How deep was his personal involvement in this business, which had earlier been outsourced to his top aide, Sharad Shetty? And if he was personally involved, did it mean more than just a side business for the D-Company? These were the questions that remained to be answered.

5

THE STORY OF CHANDILA

The scorching summer heat added to the already charged atmosphere in the desert capital-city of Jaipur, although the air had cooled off by the evening. Thousands of cricket enthusiasts, many of them dressed colourfully, with a few fanatics having painted their faces in the Indian tricolour, were cheering hysterically for their favourites among both the teams. Glued to their seats in the spectacular Sawai Mansingh Stadium in Jaipur, the frenzied crowds were completely in the dark about the real game that was going to be played that evening.

Chandila, the handsome twenty-nine-year-old cricketer from Haryana's Faridabad district, had been on the police radar ever since they began tracking Tinku Mandi's phone. Sunil Bhatia and Kiran Dhole had first led the police to Chandila, and their suspicions became stronger when they realized he was using not one or two, but four mobile phones with numbers registered in different parts of the country. Normally, celebrities including tinsel towners and leading sportspersons were known to have two numbers: one shared with the industry including the media, and the other a more private number not meant to be disclosed in the public domain. Even then, carrying four numbers was fairly unusual. One Airtel number that Chandila used was found to be subscribed in the name of a certain Hazara Singh, a resident of Ajmer, Rajasthan, who could never be traced. Another, a Vodafone number, was registered in the name of a certain Jayesh Kumar Patel, a resident of Navrangpura, Ahmedabad. However, Patel later told the police that he had never subscribed to this number and had no idea how Chandila acquired it.

In any case, investigations showed that Chandila had first fixed IPL Season 5 the previous year for Mandi. Chandila had allegedly received an amount of Rs 12 lakh from Bhatia that season, apart from expensive gifts as tokens of appreciation from a high-end optical shop in Khan Market, Delhi. However, the cash was asked to be returned due to failure to provide the requisite underperformance. Chandila had refused, not imagining that the matter would be taken up to the big bosses in Dubai, one of whom was Javed Chautani. Tinku informed Chautani of the case, and even requested that Chhota Shakeel intervene, giving him Chandila's number. The police have no record of this call, however, they do know that the money was returned by means of three post-dated cheques of Rs 4 lakh, each drawn in favour of Sunil Bhatia, and Chandila even promised that he would make up in the next season. He further promised that he would arrange for other teammates like Siddharth Trivedi and Chavan to perform for Tinku Mandi, for which he would take commission. This could possibly be Chandila's entry into broking.

However, Trivedi didn't end up fixing, but he took money from Chandila, mostly for shopping expenses, according to Ravi Sawani's report. But after the 2012 India TV sting operation that raised the match-fixing concerns for the Special Cell, Trivedi returned the money to Chandila saying he wanted no part in any fixes.

Trivedi had also been approached by undercover journalists in the sting operation, but he had turned them down. What Trivedi did do, however, was meet with Bhatia, a known bookie. He met him in 2012 along with Chandila, where Bhatia talked about fixing. When Trivedi questioned Chandila afterwards, he told Trivedi to forget about it. Trivedi would meet Bhatia again during the 2013 IPL, when the bookie would ask him to pass on a message to Chandila about returning his money for yet another non-performance.

As Chandila grew in his business, he didn't limit himself to dealing with only Tinku Mandi. There were intercepted calls that suggested Chandila was linked to another group of fixers he had got involved with through one Bhupender Nagar, whom he had met in various places in Delhi and Jaipur along with other members of Nagar's cartel, namely Vikas Chaudhury (Vicky), Nitin Jain (Susu), and Vindo Sharma (Monu). Chandila had even received Rs 15 lakh for spot-fixing in IPL from another fixer known as Deepak Kumar (Deepu).[1]

However, for now, the Tinku Mandi deal was in play via Amit Kumar Singh. The Special Cell could see from the bills at JW Marriott, Jaipur, that while Chandila was staying there with the Rajasthan Royals team, fixers Manan Bhatt and Chandresh Patel had also checked in. Manan Bhatt, ten years junior to Chandila, had befriended him in Ahmedabad. Bhatt, who was part of the 'Jeetu Tharad Pyramid', would later be the one to hook Sreesanth. The police realized fast that the underworld had dedicated various fixers to spread the net on different players, and these fixers could be based anywhere in the country.

Slowly, the web around Chandila revealed itself. In addition to Bhatia, former cricketer-turned-fixer Manish Guddewar had also played an important part in recruiting him. Guddewar, who hailed from Gadchiroli district near Nagpur and had played Ranji cricket for Vidarbha, was a phone call away from Chandila. These old connections, in this case the connection between a fellow Nagpurian (Guddewar) and a Ranji player, were important in 'comforting' the 'fixed' player.

Similarly, former player Amit Kumar Singh was connected to Chandila as well. An intercepted tape had established the comfort level between Singh and Chandila beyond doubt, and the bond had been deeper than being part of the same Rajasthan Royals team. Singh had known Chandila since the time the former's father was posted at the Air Force Station in Faridabad. According to the investigators, Chandila felt most secure in the company of Manan Bhatt, Manish Guddewar and Amit Kumar Singh.

It is easy to see why Chandila was an easy target. His journey into the world of fame had been a slow one. After years of plying his trade in Haryana and then playing club cricket in Delhi, he finally got a taste of success when he got picked for Rajasthan Royals. The Haryana spinner was included in the squad in the 2012 season and was relatively unknown, till he turned around a match at Sawai Mansingh Stadium. Coming in to bowl with a cushion of 170 to defend against a side already out of contention for the play-offs, the twenty-eight-year-old claimed New Zealand batsman Jesse Ryder off the fifth delivery of the chase. He followed it up with the wicket of Kolkata Knightriders skipper Sourav Ganguly and returned in the next over to remove Robin Uthappa, unleashing massive celebrations on and off the field.

But Chandila's antics off the field were not as admired. According to Manoj Sharma, the coach of the Air India team which Chandila represented, 'the off-spinner always had a knack for developing shady contacts'. Deepak Joon, the then Air India team captain, further confirmed this: 'There were times when he wouldn't accompany us. And people often turned up to enquire about his whereabouts as he owed them money.'

It would be his love for money that would eventually get him banned from the game.

●

Dusk had fallen on the Pink City, and the tidal wave of IPL had reached its peak. At 8 p.m. on 5 May 2013, Rajasthan Royals were scheduled to clash with Pune Warriors at the Sawai Mansingh Stadium. Just the previous month, Pune Warriors had defeated Rajasthan Royals by seven wickets, and now the Royals were looking forward to avenging that defeat.

About 277 kilometres away, in the control room of the Special Cell of the Delhi Police, audio tapes of the scripted match were being played. The police were listening to a conversation between Chandila and former cricketer Amit Kumar Singh, which confirmed that the match between the two teams was going to be a fixed one.[2]

Amit Kumar Singh: *Haan?* (Yes?)
Ajit Chandila: *Bhai, mujhe jane do, main signal de doonga.* (Bhai, let me go, I will give the signal.)
Singh: *Haan.* (OK.)
Chandila: *Pehla over toh aa jane do, main dekh loonga apne hisab se.* (Let the first over be. I will handle it my way.)
Singh: *Nahi, nahi, pehla over tera accha gaya toh . . .* (No, no . . . if your first over goes well, then . . .)
Chandila: *Pehla over mera accha jaye toh . . .* (If my first over goes well, then . . .)
Singh: *Confident rahkar ball daalna.* (Bowl with confidence.)
Chandila: *Confident hokar hi ball daalunga, per yahi toh main bol raha hun. Pehle tu bol raha hain karna hain wahan dekh kar jaakar.* (I will bowl with confidence but this is what I am saying. First you said to go there and see.)
Singh: *Tere ko malum hain na kya signal dena hain?* (You know the signal you're supposed to give, right?)
Chandila: *T-shirt ko upar karni hain aur sir niche karna hain.* (Yes, I have to pull my T-shirt up and put my head down.)
Singh: *Manan udhar hi rahega. Oos din jaisa mat karna. Theek hain, bhai?* (Manan will be there only. Don't do what you did last time. All right, bhai?)
Chandila: *Nahi, nahi. Indication dekar he hoga job. Theek hain.* (No, no . . . I will give the indication before it happens. Okay.)

As the investigators heard Singh directing Chandila to give a pre-decided signal before the second over of his spell in which he would give away more than fourteen runs, their long-standing suspicions about Chandila were confirmed. The police already had an indication that Chandila had possibly taken a sum of Rs 20 lakh as advance. Now they were keeping a watch on the crucial signal he was supposed to give the bookie.

These signals, the police would learn over the course of the investigation, were critical to the fixing world. They did not just kick off the betting, but also reassured the fixer that the player was on track and ready to deliver the goods. Different spot-fixing signals were being used by players, like rotating wrist watches, pulling T-shirts up and down, tucking a towel into their pants, or removing their chains or lockets. During the times of Azharuddin and Jadeja, the signal would be to pull out the chain locket from the T-shirt. There were some players who had superstitious tics, like Mohinder Amarnath who always had a red hanky hanging out of his pants. These indicators developed as potential signals amongst the bookies. They were innocuous signals, something players usually did as part of the game. Chandila's method was to untuck his jersey, and it was essential that he did it at the right time.

The police waited with their eyes glued to the TV screens. They waited with bated breath to see if their own innings would begin with the onset of his over.

At the stadium, when the match began, Pune Warriors were batting first, with Aaron Finch and Robin Uthappa opening for the team. Chandila started off with his slow right-arm bowling.

Off the first five balls, they scored five, and in the sixth, Finch hit him for a four, thus giving away nine runs in his first over.

As his second over approached, Manan Bhatt sat amongst the other spectators with bated breath as Chandila prepared to bowl. Would the boy deliver as promised? He looked keenly at Chandila, waiting for the signal that would tell the fixers to alert their bookie network to begin accepting bets. Minutes passed. Chandila took the ball, and without pulling out his T-shirt, launched into his second over!

Idiot! Manan Bhatt let out a string of abuses at Chandila under his breath. He was not sure if Chandila had changed his mind regarding their agreement or had simply forgotten to give the signal. Only the end of the second over would tell. But it no longer mattered in any case. The over had started, and the fixers could not get in the bets. In just a matter of minutes, they had lost several lakh rupees. Manan knew there would be hell to pay for, and Chandresh would be furious. Chandresh had already showered lavish gifts on Chandila to 'keep him happy': two expensive watches – the first a G-Shock and the second a Diesel. And his investment had backfired.

On the field, however, Chandila's game had changed. For the unsuspecting viewer it, was merely a case of irresponsible bowling, something that even the best bowlers have been known to do under stress. But this was not stress. Chandila was delivering the promised runs. In his mind, the agreement was intact. He didn't realize that the moment had been lost. He purposely bowled either too short or too full, and allowed the batsmen to hit a few boundaries, giving away fourteen runs in the second over, as had been promised to his fixers!

Chandila had proved himself loyal to the lords of betting and fixing. He had just forgotten to give the signal. Even though things hadn't gone as planned, the fixers could still use him for the match on 15 May, for which Chandila had negotiated the terms with Ankeet Chavan. But the police knew they probably couldn't make a case despite the evidence against Chandila. The signal on the field hadn't been given, so there was no proof to establish that Chandila was following a script.

Eventually, despite all the taped conversations about deals with bookies and fixers like Bhupendar Nagar from Delhi and Deepak from Punjab, the BCCI would delay taking administrative action on Chandila, who went on to proclaim his innocence, swearing that he 'and the IPL were clean'. After his arrest, he and his outraged family would claim the entire episode was just a case of 'fake news' in which he was simply 'a victim of conspiracy'. His mother would also choose to remain in denial, proclaiming in true Bollywood style that her son would never do something like this. 'I have given birth to him,' she would dramatically declare.

When the match finally got over, Rajasthan Royals' fans screamed with joy as their team defeated Pune Warriors by 5 wickets with one ball to spare. They even forgave Chandila for his poor performance in the second over.

Chandila, however, would have taken a long time to forgive himself. For a person who had sold his soul for money and betrayed the faith that people had in him, it came as a double blow when he had to return the advance of Rs 20 lakh. Not untucking his jersey would be an expensive mistake, but in retrospect, it would also be the reason no guilt could be proved against him.

6

THE ANGRY YOUNG MAN

Undeterred by the fiasco in Jaipur, bookies Chandresh Patel and Manan Bhatt were working overtime to compensate the losses incurred by them due to Chandila's mistake. They had already laid the foundation for the next Rajasthan Royals match on 9 May. This time they had a player who was more senior than Chandila, and celebrated for his talent. The bookies had 'fixed' Sreesanth.

Once again, the fixers had done their homework well. The web around the chosen player was so tightly woven that there was no doubt that the prey would be caught. The principal person for this fix would once again be the former Ranji player Amit Kumar Singh, who had fixed Chandila. But he was not speaking to Sreesanth directly. The conduit between them was a certain Jiju Janardanan.

Jiju and Sreesanth had a history that went back to their days at the MRF Pace Academy in Chennai where both of them trained during 2002–03. They bonded immediately due to their Kerala connection. Born in Kerala, Jiju was raised in Gujarat where he went on to represent the state in the under-22 team. During this time, he kept close ties with Sreesanth. Whenever Jiju visited Kerala, he would stay at Sreesanth's place in Kochi. Sreesanth always looked out for him as a brother and would introduce Jiju among his friends as such. This deep friendship was to cost Sreesanth his career.

In 2007, pinning his hopes on Sreesanth's growing influence in Kerala Cricket Association (KCA), Jiju left Gujarat for Kerala. But this move didn't help him. A KCA official was quoted by media reports that Sreesanth had tried his best to get his pal into the Ranji Trophy side. The official had said, 'Janardanan represented the Kerala Under-25 side, but he was just not good enough to play Ranji. Sreesanth spoke to us on several occasions, but we told him it wouldn't be possible as Janardanan hadn't done well in the selection games.'[1]

While Sreesanth's career went from strength to strength, Jiju's faltered and eventually came to a standstill. By the time he came to terms with the fact that he would never become a cricketer of merit, he began to leverage his contacts in Gujarat and began to set up a network with a few bookies he had met from the Saurashtra region. He eventually found a way to his old friend Amit Singh, who was now broking player deals for his own network. Amit and Jiju themselves had a shared history that traced back to the time when they had both played for Gujarat. In 2013, when Sreesanth jumped back into the game after several injuries and setbacks, Jiju introduced him to Amit in a five-star hotel.

The 1983-born starry-eyed younger son of Santhakumaran and Savithri Devi Nair, who had modelled his initial bowling style on his idol Anil Kumble, was the perfect choice for the fixers. His promising career had begun to derail, acquiring a reputation for recklessness over the years. The Indian captain M. S. Dhoni had articulated his disdain for Sreesanth's antics several times. After another of Sreesanth's rants in 2011, this time on South African captain Graeme Smith, Dhoni made amends at an ICC function and assured Smith there wouldn't be a repeat performance. However, even Dhoni endorsed Smith's view that Sreesanth was hard to control. Dhoni also held the Kerala speedster responsible for the team's slow overrate.

It was almost a given that the pacer's international career, courtesy of his injuries and poor attitude, was almost over. He had last played a Test in August 2011 and the World Cup final that year was the last ODI he had played for India. Sreesanth had not played a T20 game for India since February 2008. The IPL was all he had, and there was no doubt he would be willing to milk it in every possible way.

From being Kerala's pride to turning into cricket's enfant terrible, Sreesanth's was a career that played out under the glare of the limelight. His was not the story of the journeyman Chandila, who acquired fame a little too late and scrambled desperately to make up for lost time and money. His story was the story of a destiny's child, a recognizable talent and a distinct personality that stood out from the slew of new cricketers who flooded the nation's sports pages upon the advent of the IPL.

Sreesanth made his international debut against Sri Lanka in a Nagpur ODI on 25 October 2005, at the age of 22. Earlier, in November 2004, Sreesanth had received accolades for taking a hat-trick against Himachal Pradesh in the Ranji Trophy. In October 2005, he was Man of the Series in the Challenger Trophy, a domestic limited-overs tournament where he was the leading wicket-taker with the third-best bowling average. This was his ticket to the Indian team for the home ODI series against Sri Lanka. He then went on to be a part of the Indian team which won the first T20 World Cup in 2007 and the fifty-over World Cup in 2011. Many thought that luck was in his favour, as he was selected to the Indian team while S. K. Nair, a Keralite, was BCCI secretary. And when he caught the ball to dismiss Misbah-ul-Haq in the 2007 T20 World Cup finals, his friends and his doting brother Deepu had branded Sreesanth as a lucky mascot for India. Jokes began to circulate that one could hit a ball anywhere in the world, and one would find a Malayali to catch it.

But Sreesanth quickly acquired an unpleasant reputation. In a 2006 Test match against South Africa, he was fined 30 per cent of his match fee after he pleaded guilty to breaching the ICC Code of Conduct on two counts. In 2007, during Australia's tour of India, Sreesanth again courted controversy, rubbing Australia's Andrew Symonds the wrong way on a couple of occasions during that tour. Apparently, during a game that he wasn't playing, Sreesanth ran inside the ground with drinks the moment Symonds got out, and sledged him.[2]

But his most public spat came during the inaugural IPL in 2008, when he was slapped by Harbhajan Singh – apparently Sreesanth had provoked the off-spinner – at the end of the match between Kings XI and Mumbai Indians. Harbhajan was fined heavily and banned from the tournament, but it was Sreesanth who got a bad name because his reputation as the 'angry young man of cricket' had already been established. In 2013, Sreesanth described that incident in a Twitter rant, saying that he was never slapped and that Bhajji was a 'back-stabber'. Later, he deleted all those tweets.

For right or the wrong reasons, Sreesanth was certainly grabbing headlines. With both his popularity and notoriety graph on the rise, some film-makers also made a beeline to rope in the pacer and superstar Mammootty together. And Kerala couldn't get over her golden son! The locality in which he lived in Kochi before shifting to a gated community was renamed from Kailash Nagar to Sreesanth Nagar, before the change ran into some legal issues. For a football-crazy state, Kerala embraced its most famous cricketer with love and affection.

Sreesanth lapped it all up – fame, money, women, the good life. His penchant for spending and his lavish lifestyle made headline news, especially the famous Rs 1.93 lakh single transaction with Diesel. The bookies too would learn how to keep their star performer particularly happy by giving him the kind of women he liked. Manan Bhatt and Chandresh did this for him on at least three known occasions, and a video tape from a Chandigarh hotel of him frolicking with unknown women, even as he was engaged to his long-time girlfriend Bhuvneshwari Kumari Shekhavat from the Jaipur royal family, would make the news.

It would eventually be his love for the fast life that would lead to his downfall.

Three days before the match was to be played, on 6 May, at 5:40 p.m., investigators sat glued to their chairs with headphones wired into the recording devices of the Special Cell, and realized that Sreesanth had indeed been bought by the fixers. Jiju had taken delivery of Rs 10 lakh in cash as advance for spot-fixing for the 9 May match from Chandresh Patel at JW Marriott Hotel in Jaipur. Once again, the deal was to deliver 14 runs during his second over. As the tapes began to record, the investigators heard Sreesanth and Jiju speaking in Malayalam, where the former wanted to gift expensive mobiles to two of his girlfriends – Sakshi Jhala and Deepika. (Incidentally, it was Sakshi Dhoni who had introduced Sreesanth to one of these girls.)[3] Here's the translated version:

Sreesanth: Hello?

Jiju: I'm in the room.

Sreesanth: Don't go with that fatso, you go in alone.

Jiju: Who the hell is going with him? I am going alone.

Sreesanth: Buy three phones.

Jiju: Okay. You need three? Let me see how much I am getting from them. Why do you want to spend all the money now? We have got 10 now. I will take 3 and the 7 remains here. Let me know when you want it.

Sreesanth: Take 1 [lakh] and buy three phones.

Jiju: If we are getting from there, we should buy. Let's see. Save some money.

Sreesanth: Oh, why don't you buy them now?

Jiju: Okay. That boy is meeting me. I'll bring over three phones. Let me know which colour you want.

Sreesanth: Let's meet around 8:30 p.m. in the room. Then we shall go to the office.

Jiju: Office?

Sreesanth: I mean that orphanage.

Jiju: Okay, 8:30 p.m. Come, I also have a phone.

Sreesanth: Okay, bye.

Jiju: Okay, bye. I will get some money if I manage to get a contract.

Sreesanth: Yes? Which one?

Jiju: Some company. There is good money if I can bag this company contract.

Sreesanth: Yes.

Jiju: Funds can be given by your sister, right?

Sreesanth: God will help.

Jiju: Okay.

In the tape, Jiju could be heard performing his role as a broker for Sreesanth for both legal and illegal contracts. While Jiju was very clear about taking his 3 lakh out of the 10 lakh, he had a word of caution for Sreesanth, which Sreesanth blithely ignored. Jiju then went on to disobey Sreesanth's instructions and spent only Rs 50,000 rather than a lakh.

At 8:32 p.m., Jiju went to Jaipur's Crystal Palm Mall to buy the phones. There was another call:

Jiju: You need two Z10, right?

Sreesanth: Yes, buy two of them.

Jiju: But I don't have enough money for two.

Sreesanth: I told you to take 1 [lakh] with you.

Jiju: I went to get 1 but got only 50. What should I buy – Bold 4 or Z10? Should I buy one Z10?

Sreesanth: You said Bold 4. Hence, I took this.

Sreesanth: Oh, you have one Z10?

Jiju: Yes, when do you have to give it, tomorrow?

Sreesanth: I want to give it today.

Jiju: Okay. Let it be with whatever I have in hand.

Sreesanth: Are you crazy?

Jiju: Oh, God!

Sreesanth: Arrey, didn't I tell you to take along 1 lakh rupees?

Jiju: Okay, whatever I said was wrong. Now I am coming along with the phone.

Sreesanth: Arrey, but how can you get it?

Jiju: I am buying it no matter what.

●

On the day of the match at PCA Stadium in Mohali, the crowd erupted in applause when Rahul Dravid, Captain of Rajasthan Royals, entered the arena. Everyone in the stadium knew that the iconic cricketer had a big role to play in the fortunes of his team, which had missed the knockout stages in the last four seasons, but this year, they had finally pulled themselves up under Dravid's leadership. The future of the team was riding on this day's match. If they won against Kings XI, they would be in the play-offs – their first since 2008. Dravid had put in blood and sweat to make his team one of the best in IPL 6.

As the music blared through the speakers and fans cheered hoarsely, Dravid won the toss and chose to bowl, saying the pitch was a little dry and could ease out later. The game began. Meanwhile, the investigators also began their long vigil on the TV screens.

Like in the case of Chandila, Sreesanth's first over was above reproach. In fact, he bowled almost flawlessly, allowing Marsh and Gilchrist no more than 5 runs. But, like Chandila, his game changed in the second over.

As per the plan, Sreesanth was to give a signal before bowling the over: he would tuck in his hand-towel into his trousers. He would also buy the bookies some time by doing extended stretching exercises before delivering this over.

Which is what he exactly did. As the match played itself out in Mohali, the TV sets in the Special Cell were beaming out the images that had been conjured in the minds of the investigators by what they had heard over the phone calls. On the field, Sreesanth gave the pre-decided signal and did his stretches before he began bowling the second over. But despite his best intentions, Sreesanth's plans went awry. The deal was to give 14 runs in this over, but he managed to give away three fours and one single – 13 runs, one short than the promised number!

As the police watched the replays repeatedly, all the images from Sreesanth's previously illustrious career suddenly seemed to get blurred as their eyes kept returning to the right pocket of his blue trousers, where a white towel hung, neatly tucked in place. The police were certain that what they had heard on the tapes and watched on the television screen had converged. The clip where Sreesanth tucked in his towel and bowled the compromised over would be recorded as evidence in the eventual case against him, and also become one of the most viewed clips on the internet.[4]

There was tension in the air later that night. Sreesanth had done everything that was asked apart from giving away one run less; there was no doubt that Sreesanth had performed 'well'. He had proved himself to be a player, on whom money could be safely bet upon. This would go on to pave the way for another big fix in less than a week – on 15 May. But the kingpins weren't going to let the one run go away so easily. While the Rs 10 lakh advance had been given, the rest of the Rs 50 lakh they had agreed upon in offline conversations was now in jeopardy.

In a subsequent telephone conversation on the evening of 9 May between Jiju and Amit, the former was heard defending Sreesanth and trying to wheedle some more money out of the latter, since he perceived the full payment wouldn't come through. What was more unnerving in this call was hearing a bookie almost demanding a ball-by-ball justification from one of India's most promising bowlers and dictating his play with the full authority of a person who now owns his talent:[5]

Jiju: Hello.

Amit Kumar Singh: I have talked to them.

Jiju: *Haan*. (Okay)

Amit: We are in losses. I had told you earlier that 13 is also a loss. Only 14 and above is profitable.

Jiju: Yes, that's right.

Amit: I told them that he [Sreesanth] has worked hard, so something should be done and they said they will do it after the match.

Jiju: Sreesanth has kept his word, right?

Amit: They are saying they have lost. It happens as per the calculation of that particular session.

Jiju: No, no, there is no doubt that Sreesanth kept his word. Have you seen the entire match?

Amit: You had told Sree, right? What did you tell him?

Jiju: I had cleared everything with him.

Amit: Why didn't he just bowl a wide ball?

Jiju: He bowled a wide one towards the end, but Gilchrist hit that for a 4. Sree gave a wide ball, he hit a four and Shaun Marsh faced it. He bowled a no-ball as well as a full toss.

Amit: Okay, I understand. I am fighting . . .

Jiju: He bowled a short ball and a full ball too, but that guy didn't hit at all. No, no, there is no room for doubt. Everything was cleared. He bowled the last ball as a wide but Gilchrist hit a four off it. He – Sree – tried his level best. Unfortunately, two balls went as dot balls and we fell one run short.

Amit: I am making things clear to these people, but they are firm that they have lost money. I want some time to talk to them, I will get back.

Jiju: Okay, you will not take back what you have given, right?

Amit: No, man, we have to work together again. That's the advance.

Jiju: No, that is over. He will not get it . . . I am not asking for 5 or 6 more . . . that will be wrong. I know Sree very well. If those guys give him 2 or 5, that should satisfy Sree.

Amit: Tell Sree that they are running into losses; Amit is trying. Why don't you find out the losses . . .

Jiju: That's obvious.

Amit: You don't need to give any justification.

Jiju: They have seen the match, everything was all right.

Amit: I told them that if they don't give any money, it's their loss. This guy is always with you. It's a long-term relationship; it will not come to an end in one day! I am trying. You just stay calm, I will do something.

The story of Sreesanth had become a validation of the old adage: cheaters never prosper. During the raids conducted in the aftermath of his arrest, the remaining money (Rs 5.5 lakh from his friend Abhishek Shukla's house) was recovered by the police.[6] All Sreesanth got from maligning the sport; tainting the IPL and surrendering his soul were a couple of expensive phones and a sackful of designer clothes. If his spot-fixing career would not have been cut short, who knows if it would really have paid off in the end? If the confessions of Jiju are to be believed, Sreesanth would have gotten into more trouble the deeper he went. Jiju and other members of the syndicate were planning to make sex video clips of him with an escort in a Mumbai hotel. Jiju, according to the police sources, reportedly told Delhi Police that they postponed the making of the video. According to him, this honey trap was a common way of holding cricketers to ransom and had been done to a few already. In view of this, it can be said that things could have been a lot worse for the angry young cricketer. The sex tapes may have put a grinding halt to his wedding, which finally took place in 2013 to Bhuvneshwari, who came out in public in support of him despite all the escorts and unknown women he had been with. By getting caught when he did, Sreesanth may have been ruined professionally, but his personal life was salvaged.

7

THE EDGY BOOKIE

It remains unclear how much money Sreesanth finally received from the betting syndicate, but thanks to his efforts in the match on 9 May,, the syndicate knew they'd got him on their side. Their interpretation of the events veered more towards 'bad luck' than towards any purposeful violation of the contract. They knew Sreesanth was their man and would do whatever he was asked to do, whenever he was asked to do. No problems were anticipated. But the problem of under-delivering on the runs still remained.

Added to this was Chandila's previous act of omission by not giving a pre-decided signal to the fixer. These episodes had made Chandresh Patel furious, as the bookies could not book the session for making windfall gains. The situation was tough for someone in Chandresh's position – not only would he have to explain the financial loss, he would also have to work harder to keep the faith of the network for future matches. The biggest challenge for the bookies was to hedge against the risks even when they had fixed players. The anxiety was about erroneous delivery on agreed terms and lack of certainty or precise delivery.

Chandila's and Sreesanth's failures had sent waves of unease down the fixing network. The fact that Chandila had not delivered as per the bookies' expectations in the 2012 IPL too was not conducive for the bookies to depend on the player's underperformance. As stakes were higher compared to normal betting volumes, the bookies were becoming overcautious. Now they were edgy about their future earnings. What if another of the 'fixed' players didn't deliver? Was their money safe in the hands of the promises made by Chandresh?

An intercepted voice call between Chandresh Patel and a bookie showed the nervousness that was seeping through the ranks at this time, and the effort that Chandresh put to reassure the bookie that Sreesanth would perform on demand. The extremely edgy bookie was worried about the next match that was fixed – the one taking place on 15 May 2013 in Mumbai between Rajasthan Royals and Mumbai Indians. The bookie, as can be seen in the transcripts, was worried about the delivery of runs and the order of the fixed overs, and was being told by an extremely exasperated Chandresh that Sreesanth would deliver in all possible scenarios. It's interesting to note the repetition, and the iron-clad guarantees that the bookie seemed to want from Chandresh. We can hear Chandresh adding his Rs 5 crore bet possibly as a sign of faith.

On the other hand, the call also went on to show how much control Chandresh wielded over Chandila and Sreesanth. But this 'control' had to be conveyed down the line to the bookies to encourage them to take bets.

This call was intercepted at 1:35 p.m., a few hours before a match between Rajasthan Royals and Chennai Super Kings was to be played on 12 May at Jaipur:

Unidentified Bookie: Brother, first listen to me. I've come again to eat your brain.

Chandresh: Yaar, *bhain*****, are you sick or what?

Bookie: Arrey, one minute, I want to explain.

Chandresh: *Chhote mein baat hain kya?* (Will this be in brief?)

Bookie: No, man. Now I won't talk again. In the first one, [if] our favourite Chandila [bowls], bet only then. If tomorrow someone else does the second over and then again the fourth? I'm telling you.

Chandresh: *Haan.*

Bookie: That's what I've come to ask. First is done but what if he doesn't do it in the second and somebody else comes, then the runs will come only in the third over. This is the deal with Sreesanth, right?

Chandresh: *Haan.*

Bookie: Then whatever happens later, at least our runs will come in the third. Do you want to cut your ticket or wait for it to come in the fourth? [Meaning: Do you want to stop or continue betting?]

Chandresh: No, not then, if that figure comes, then cut it. Means, suppose you put 60, then do 60 . . .

Bookie: So should I cut yours too?

Chandresh: Yes, mine too.

Bookie: So should I call and tell them that we have put it in the third?

Chandresh: You don't need to call. If we get 60, mine will automatically get cut. You also cut yours, there's no problem in that.

Bookie: Then Sreesanth won't do it later.

Chandresh: Man, even if he does, who'll know when it comes?

Bookie: Then we won't come to know.

Chandresh: He will do it again, he will definitely do it in the second.

Bookie: Yeah, but then how will you let me know? I'm asking you only about Sreesanth . . .

Chandresh: He will do it in the second, that's final.

Bookie: OK, so Sreesanth will do it in his second over, whenever it comes. So should I place yours?

Chandresh: Yes, yes, yes. This is only how the third and fourth will come! You're really confusing things. The third and fourth will come . . .

Bookie: Third and fourth will only come . . .

Chandresh: *Haan.*

Bookie: Means, he does the first, he does the second . . .

Chandresh: *Arrey, ma ch*** yaar*!

Bookie: I've cut that much, then if it doesn't happen, it will be less.

Chandresh: It will come in the third, fourth, the matter is finished. If in the first, only both of them get runs, then it's another matter.

Bookie: Hoon, hoon, hullo . . .

Chandresh: *Haan, haan* . . .

Bookie: First he will do, second he will do, then we should put it from the fourth ball only. But if the session comes, then I will cut 40 for you too.

Chandresh: *Haan, haan.* (Okay).

Bookie: If someone else comes in the third, you have to cut 60 only. No figure for you . . .

Chandresh: *Haan, haan.*

Bookie: Then just as someone else comes in the fourth over, Sreesanth will come in the ninth over and do?

Chandresh: Yes, even then he will do it.

Bookie: Then should I do yours?

Chandresh: Yes, do it.

Bookie: Just listen to me. Phone me and put 5 crore, then I will understand.

Chandresh: I don't put on outgoing, brother.

Bookie: (Static)

Chandresh: Is the line okay?

Bookie: Five means if our work is not done in the fourth, then your 5? Is that okay?

Chandresh: OK, OK.

●

Till date it has still not been established who this bookie was, but Chandresh's position at this time was clear. He had fixed two players to perform for him in the forthcoming match – Chandila and Sreesanth. His confidence that both of them would perform as per his demand was clear throughout the call. This call was also illustrative of the fact that all of the accused were attempting to fix matches throughout the tournament, and the syndicate was prematurely terminated when they were arrested by the Special Cell.

However, to the detriment of the syndicate and to the benefit of Rajasthan Royals (which went on to win the match), both players were not selected in the final eleven. Chandila, despite not delivering on two occasions, was still a priority for Chandresh. He had gone out of his way to take care of Chandila's needs as he had to use him to engage with other players. The survival of their business depended on more players coming in, especially as Chandila was unable to deliver as per their expectations, and also because he and Ankeet Chavan had been dropped from two matches, during which they were allegedly supposed to concede a certain number of runs. On Chandresh's request, however, Chandila contacted his teammates Brad Hodge, Kevin Cooper and Siddharth Trivedi, though to no avail because the three players did not show any interest.[1]

Chandila and the Rajasthan Royals team were not the only things that were giving Chandresh Patel sleepless nights.

Another startling revelation that came out after Chandresh's arrest was that the bookies were trying to fix a second team other than Rajasthan Royals. If his statement was to be believed, the three players, all belonging to Rajasthan Royals, who had been arrested by the Delhi Police could have involved more teams had they had it their way.

While Chandresh was arrested by the Delhi Police in connection with spot-fixing, he would also be taken into custody by the Mumbai Crime Branch to investigate the betting case against Gurunath Meiyappan, Vindoo Dara Singh and others.

Chandresh alleged that he had met Sunrisers Hyderabad players to fix their match against Pune Warriors to be held on 17 April that year. The deal was reportedly fixed by a man named Amir, who had approached the bookies and offered to fix the match. Amir had told the bookies that in order to fix the match he would require Rs 6 crore, of which 5 crores would go to the players while the rest would be taken as commission by Amir himself. Chandresh claimed that three days before the match, he had met some of the Sunrisers players and finalized the deal, wherein the players, in return, would lose the match against Pune Warriors. The arrangement was that Sunrisers would not score more than 120 runs in the match and, while batting, would lose one of their wickets in the second over of their innings.

In retrospect, the first innings of the match went exactly as the bookies had planned – a Sunrisers batsman got out off the last ball of the second over, and the team went on to score 119 runs, thus giving a target of 120 to Pune Warriors, who duly won the match.

On the basis of this revelation, certain phone numbers belonging to Amir, whose real name was M. D. Shakil, and his associates, including a Mohammed Yahiya (Yusuf), began to be tapped. On 24 May, Yahiya was arrested from the Hyderabad International Airport while trying to escape to Dubai. He was eventually found to be involved in spot-fixing. Then on 26 May, one more accused, namely Babu Sunil Chander Saxena, was arrested from Hyderabad. He was also found to be working with Yahiya for Amir. On 27 May, another man called Syed Durrey Ahmed (Shoaib) was arrested, again from Hyderabad, for working with Amir.

But what about the Sunrisers Hyderabad throwing away a match? The Mudgal Committee, investigating the whole scandal, had touched upon this and questioned whether in addition to Rajasthan Royals and Chennai Super Kings, one more IPL team had fallen prey to fixing, but since proof was missing no conclusive charges were framed.

8

FIRST-TIMER CHAVAN

On the afternoon of 15 May 2013, a few hours before the Rajasthan Royals versus Mumbai Indians match, the bookies learnt that Sreesanth and Chandila were both being dropped from the game. Their two favourite boys were gone! Replacements had to be quickly made.

Then on the same afternoon, the police managed to intercept a call at 2:24 p.m. between Amit Singh and fixer-cum-bookie Jitender Kumar Jain. The call confirmed their worst suspicions: another player had fallen for the lure. This one was the most surprising:

Jitender: Hello.

Amit Singh: Jitubhai, Amit speaking.

Jitender: Yes, tell me, Amit bhaiyya.

Amit: Now Sreesanth is not playing. Ankeet is playing. But he is taking time. We are trying. If it happens, I'll let you know but keep your expectations down.

Jitender: It's okay, I'm not coming.

Amit: You don't get out. I'm meeting him in the evening.

Jitender: Is Watson playing or not?

Amit: Yes, he is. I'm also meeting Sreesanth in the evening.

Jitender: OK, it doesn't matter.

Amit: I'll do something and come, brother. Don't take tension . . . he is ready to work.

Jitender: You're speaking on our behalf, Amit bhaiyya. We don't even get to talk to you.

Amit: I'll manage something and let you know after the evening's meeting.

Jitender: No problem.

Amit was determined to 'fix' someone in the match and had his eyes on Ankeet. Talks with Ankeet had been going on for a while, but the boy was yet to succumb. He had been hanging around Sreesanth and Chandila a lot more, as the statement of Rajasthan Royals player Siddharth Trivedi would later reveal:

'In the recently concluded session of IPL, I had observed that Sreesanth, Ankeet Chavan, Owais Shah, Dishant Yagnik, Stuart Binny, Ajit Chandila, Samuel Badri, Jiju and Abhishek had become best friends and always used to go out partying together. I do not know what they used to do during their outings or parties but whenever they invited me to join them, I used to decline as I was busy attending to my wife who is pregnant.'[1]

The fixers were desperate. Ankeet didn't really fit the profile of the greedy, flashy youngster as Sreesanth and Chandila had.

As Harmeet Singh of Rajasthan Royals would reveal later in a recorded statement, the fixers had been willing to approach anyone and were desperately looking for names even before the news of Chandila and Sreesanth being dropped was declared. According to Harmeet, they had asked for Watson and Ajinkya Rahane, but Chandila had said they wouldn't do it, but Ankeet might.[2]

So the fixers got working on Ankeet. In March 2013, Ankeet met with bookies Tinku Mandi and Kiran Dhole in Delhi near Hotel Ashoka. Ankeet was staying in Hotel Ashoka with his brother Nihar Anil Chavan (a crew-member with Air India). Their mobile call details would later show they were constantly in touch during this period.

The story of Ankeet Chavan's fall couldn't be more different than his two teammates. If Sreesanth was an attention seeker who was 'an accident waiting to happen' and Chandila was a smart-talking opportunist, Ankeet was a child gone astray. A Ruparel College boy, he grew up in a *chawl* in Matunga and had been a disciplined and humble cricketer. According to the Mumbai under-19 coach Satish Samant, who had trained him in the late 90s and known him for fifteen years, Ankeet was a 'sincere' cricketer who wanted to work his way up to the top through hard work. Ashish Patankar, the MIG Cricket Club secretary, recalled scolding Ankeet as a schoolboy once for bowling 'horribly' in one over. 'He never repeated that. He is a hardworking cricketer,' said Patankar.

Ankeet's rise in Mumbai cricket was gradual, similar to that of some of his predecessors like Nilesh Kulkarni, Ravi Thakkar and Sanjay Patil. He had to fight for a place in the team with other left-arm spinners like Iqbal Abdullah, Gaurav Jathar and Harmeet

Singh, all-India Under-19 players. Once Abdullah's form dipped, the Mumbai selectors offered Ankeet a chance. He scored some useful runs and convinced the discerning men that he was a perfect fit for first-class and limited-over matches.

After donning the lion crest for two consecutive seasons, Chavan appeared to have cemented his place in the Mumbai team. He took nine second-innings wickets against Punjab at the Wankhede in December 2012 and had made an unbeaten 102 in trying conditions against Madhya Pradesh in January 2012 at Indore. A promising player with a middling collection of thirty-three wickets and 227 runs from ten matches, he played a crucial role in Mumbai winning the Ranji Trophy for the fortieth time the previous season. His awe-inspiring figures of 9-23 against Punjab made Harbhajan Singh declare he was the best left-arm spinner in the country. Things were shaping up well for the soft-spoken player who had won Dravid's confidence while playing for Rajasthan Royals.

Nothing in Ankeet's career or personality hinted that he was about to take a leap to the other side. Moreover, unlike the other two players, he didn't have any old relationships with any of the fixers, so perhaps his reluctance to agree stemmed from a basic lack of trust. It's not known whether the bookies upped the money, making him an offer too good to refuse, or if Chandila strong-armed him, or whether the very fact that his senior colleagues were involved gave him the confidence that he would be safe. To a rookie like Ankeet, the offence wouldn't have seemed that serious; he may have thought spot-fixing was a minor thing that wouldn't change the outcome of the match. The fact that the outcome of the match is rarely affected by spot-fixing can be a powerful argument to persuade someone who has no idea what he is getting into and what the consequences are. To a kid, it almost seems like 'money for nothing'.

On 15 May, exactly an hour after Jitendra Jain was told by Amit Singh it would be tough to get Ankeet to agree, he got another call, this time from Chandresh Patel. At 3:28 p.m., the master bookie conveyed some good news to Jain:

Chandresh: *Kaha hain?* (Where are you?)

Jitender: Palitana.

Chandresh: Palitana? Go to Ahmedabad? I'm hearing things.

Jitender: What happened?

Chandresh: Ankeet is confirmed.

Jitender: No, he's not going to do it!

Chandresh: No, no – he himself called to say he will do it. Ajit is with him and Ajit told him he had to do it and just like that it was done. That's why I'm talking to you.

Jitender: I'm not going to be able to reach in time.

Chandresh: You won't reach?

Jitender: I missed my train in the rush.

Chandresh: At least Varun bhai is there, right?

Jitender: Varun has gone to Kolkata.

Chandresh: Get Pintu or Naresh bhai. You tell Naresh bhai, but you stay on the phone.

Jitender: No problem.

The police who had been listening to the conversations in real time now knew that Ankeet was 'in play'. They now needed corroboration from Ankeet himself and very soon, at 3:31 p.m., they got the evidence that nailed Ankeet Chavan – the negotiated monies as well the signal for the bookies:

Ankeet: *Haan*, Ajit.

Chandila: *Haanji*, sir.

Ankeet: *Bolo*, sir. *Kahan par hain?* (Tell me, sir. Where are you?)

Chandila: I'm in the room.

Ankeet: OK, OK, I'd gone out for a bit.

Chandila: *Accha*. (OK.)

Ankeet: Tell me.

Chandila: You'll do it, right?

Ankeet: Yes, but the amount you told me then, right?

Chandila: 12

Ankeet: You told me more over there.

Chandila: No, I've told him.

Ankeet: OK, that's fine.

Chandila: So I've told him and it's done.

Ankeet: OK, that's fine.

Chandila: Yes, and I've told him 60.

Ankeet: Yes.

Chandila: So it's a done deal?

Ankeet: *Haan*.

Chandila: You will turn the wristband.

Ankeet: *Haan, haan*.

Chandila: If you're doing 9 or 10, still do it. And in the power play also, do it.

Ankeet: What, what?

Chandila: Do it in the power play.

Ankeet: I'll BBM this.

Chandila: *Power play mein kar diyo . . . ho gaya tera.* (If you do it in the Powerplay, you're settled.)

Ankeet: Only that?

Chandila: I've understood, I've forgotten.

Ankeet: OK.

Chandila: OK.

Police Commissioner Neeraj Kumar did not waste a moment in dispatching special teams to Mumbai to be part of the spectators in the stadium. Another team was already assigned the task of monitoring and recording the live coverage of the match from the control room. If the action on the field matched the conversation they had just heard, they would finally have enough evidence to begin the arrests.

The summer heat was building up at the crowded Wankhede Stadium even though it was almost night. But the crowd didn't care. This was their favourite Mumbai Indians playing on their home ground in an iconic stadium. The match was sure to be memorable even if Sachin Tendulkar wasn't there to make it unforgettable. The Master Blaster was missing because of a tendon problem.

At 7:30 p.m. on 15 May, out on the field, Dravid won the toss for Rajasthan Royals and chose to bowl. Ankeet opened the innings with an almost perfect over. He gave away just 2 runs. Then, a rerun of the same drama that had played twice earlier happened, when Ankeet started to bowl his second over. The signal had come through, and the bowler began his over.

Right on, the first ball was a six. The crowd went mad cheering for their beloved team. On every ball except the last one, Ankeet gave away runs and even got hit for another six off the third ball. He ended this 'fixed' over giving away 15 runs, one more than had been agreed upon with his handler, Chandila. The first-timer had outperformed old hands like Chandila and Sreesanth when it came to fixing! Not only had he remembered to give the signal, unlike Chandila, but he had also delivered on his brief, unlike Sreesanth.

At 8:19 p.m., minutes after Ankeet's delivery had set the cash registers ringing at the betting syndicate, congratulatory phone calls were being exchanged. A taped call would later show Chandila was jubilant at his own performance in netting Ankeet and couldn't wait to get his hands on the money:

Ajit Chandila: Are you happy, boss?

Manan Bhatt: Yes, yes, very happy.

Chandila: OK, so then speak to them.

Manan: I'll speak after the session, OK?

Chandila: Soon, through Amit's hands.

Manan: *Haan*, what?

Chandila: It shouldn't go to his hands. The stuff should reach me.
Manan: All right, it will happen as you wish.

This call was possibly the last piece of evidence clocked by the police before they began the arrests that very night. Between the nights of 15 and 16 May, police teams carried out simultaneous raids in Delhi and Mumbai. In their very first attempt, the Mumbai team arrested seven individuals – Ajit Chandila, Ankeet Chavan, S. Sreesanth, Amit Kumar Singh, Jiju Janardhanan, Manan Bhatt and Chandresh Patel.

When the news of the arrests reached the media, the nation would react in shock to the news of the scandal. Ankeet's involvement in particular would be met with disbelief. Unlike Sreesanth, who would later say that he wanted to make a movie out of his experiences, Ankeet would only dream about having the chance to play again. According to his lawyer Rajiv Dwivedi, Ankeet was at heart a simple *chawl*-boy: 'Ankeet may have lived in fancy hotels as a cricketer, but he comes from a typical Maharashtrian family, which is simple, and has very modest means. He is stunned at what has happened to him, but he has not complained about a single thing while in police custody. He says they have treated him well.'[3] Even the Mumbai Police, who had all three boys in custody, said that Ankeet was 'quiet and childlike' unlike Chandila, who was a 'tough nut to crack'.

But these differences didn't matter. History would forever slot Ankeet as a 'tainted player' in the same league as Sreesanth, Cronje, Azhar, Manoj Prabhakar, Ajay Jadeja and any other player who had compromised his game for money.

9

THE ARRESTS

Rajasthan Royals slumped to a 14-run loss against Mumbai Indians that night. Immediately after the match, following Ankeet's performance, calls from the bookies and fixers congratulating each other started to pour in. The cops finally had enough incriminating evidence to nail the three cricketers who were celebrating their 'fixed' performance despite the loss.

The first arrests took place late that night. Cops in plain clothes visited the Trident Hotel where the Rajasthan Royals players were staying and requested a startled Ankeet and Chandila to accompany them to the Marine Drive police station for inquiry. Sreesanth, however, was not there. He was staying in the Sofitel Hotel, nearly twenty kilometres away in Bandra Kurla complex, along with Jiju. While his team was playing at Wankhede, Sreesanth and Jiju went partying to RGs, a pub in South Mumbai. The fast bowler had no idea that his life, as he wanted it, would change forever that night.

Much like Sreesanth's career, his arrest wasn't free of drama. He was with one of his many 'female friends' in an SUV outside a five-star hotel in Mumbai when a Delhi Police team intercepted them. Sreesanth was drunk and, according to the police, began to shout and claim that he had close connections with the Kerala and Maharashtra chief ministers. In his typical brashness, he also handed over his phone to the police officers asking them to call the chief ministers.

As the television headlines began to blare the breaking news, cricket fans could not believe what they saw: big, bold scrolls screaming 'Ajit Chandila and Ankeet Chavan detained by the police in Mumbai over allegations of spot-fixing'.

Even the Rajasthan Royals team management was caught off guard by the arrests, and made no delay in proclaiming they stood on the side of the law and had no idea about the dirty players. 'We have been informed that three of our players have been called in for investigation on charges of spot-fixing in matches. We are completely taken by surprise,'[1] said a Rajasthan Royals spokesperson. 'We do not have the full facts at this point and are unable to confirm anything. We are in touch with the BCCI on this matter. We will fully cooperate with the authorities to ensure a thorough investigation. The management at Rajasthan Royals has a zero-tolerance approach to anything that is against the spirit of the game.'[2]

The three players were charged under Indian Penal Code sections 420 and 120B, which deal with offences related to cheating and criminal conspiracy, respectively. Shortly after, the stringent Maharashtra Control of Organized Crime Act

(MCOCA) was also slapped on them, given the underworld connection. Chandila was shocked that the Delhi Police had slapped MCOCA against him and pleaded that he was a 'cricketer' and 'not a terrorist'. 'My family and I are in a state of shock that such charges are being levelled against me,'[3] said Chandila two weeks after his arrest, when he was on a three-day bail to attend the last rites of his elder brother.

N. Srinivasan, the BCCI president, said the incident had come as 'a bolt from the blue',[4] while Neeraj Kumar, the Delhi Police Commissioner, furnished details of the three matches that had come under the scanner at a press conference later that day. The police had also seized all the networking devices that worked as the betting exchange from Mumbai and Delhi. They included, amongst other things, fifty mobile phones, six laptops, an iPad, a Dish TV set-top box, three Internet cards, three Wi-Fi routers, a printer, the TV decoder of Set Max, a 40-inch LCD, handwritten diaries, and papers.

The arrests created a furore in the cricketing world. The IPL had always been a subject of controversy and criticism, but cricket lovers had perhaps forgotten about match-fixing after the Azharuddin and Hansie Cronje sagas at the turn of the century. The average cricket lover seemed to have put the worst about cricket behind him. They had perhaps not imagined match-fixing would rear its head once again in a manner that would not only let them down but also shame them for calling themselves a cricket lover.

Meanwhile, news channels continued to beam images of Sreesanth with that white towel tucked into his trousers, giving away 13 of the 14 runs he had promised. That image came to represent all that was wrong with the IPL. Cricket lovers and the average Indian were amazed to hear stories about the flamboyant Chandila, and how he had lived off the bookies' money, availing of expensive watches, sun glasses, air travel, hotel stay, and so on.

At 6:45 p.m. of 14 May 2013, the crime branch rang the doorbell of Room No. 27 on the second floor of Lalwani Mansion. A middle-aged person opened the door. His name was Ramesh Vyas, who was arrested right there, in the old commercial district of Mumbai, a few furlongs away from the famous Mumba Devi temple. When the details of his arrest came out, it would lay bare the entire fixing scandal with its underworld connections in no uncertain terms. Just as Tinku Mandi was the key bookie from Delhi, Ramesh Vyas was the fulcrum in Mumbai. Vyas was the guy who dons and their key men like Firoz would speak to.

Sub-inspector Laxmikant Naryanrao Salunkhe, who was attached to the Property Cell of the Detection Crime Branch of the Mumbai Police and was keeping a tab on the bookies' activities, had no doubt that the small room in the old Kalbadevi building was being used as a betting den that had direct contacts with underworld elements from Pakistan and Dubai. Flashing their identity cards, the police shoved Vyas aside and forced themselves in only to find a television set beaming the ongoing cricket match between Royal Challengers and Kings XI. Two men were busy taking bets on mobile phones and making entries in laptops: forty-one-year-old Pandurang Govind Kadamand and thirty-two-year-old Ashok Lajpat Rai Vyas.

A piece of paper with several national and international numbers scribbled on it was tucked under several cell phones – some thirty of them – which were strewn all over their work table, many of them ringing incessantly, one after the other. The room buzzed with the continuous clatter of the phones. The betters were indeed keeping these bookies busy. One of the policemen surged ahead and switched on a phone speaker. The conversation began to rattle with names like P. Jaipur, Bunty Jaipur, Lokesh Delhi, Master Jaipur, Kothari, Bablu, Ketan, K. P. Badri, Vicky, A. A., Jupiter, Shoban, Paresh, and Lotus. The line most repeated in these conversations was, *Bhai, kya bhav chalu hain? Kitna khaya, lagaya?* (Brother, what is the going rate? How much did you put?)

Vyas, who was a resident of the Om Darya Mahal building in the posh Nepean Sea Road area, instantly confessed they were taking bets on the match working in tandem with bookies in India, Pakistan and Dubai. The bookies were quite an organized lot. There were several chits that listed phone numbers neatly written against code names or nicknames. A cursory glance at the names or their apparent origin would not reveal the bookies' true identities. For instance, common place Indian names like Shakti, Veeru, Vicky, Kaka, Vikas, Tinu, GM and U. B. L. Kisna were code names for bookies based in Pakistan, while Kamlesh, Bablu and Doctor were bookies based in Dubai.

Just as the fixers were well-informed 'doctors' of the game of cricket, the bookies were excellent accountants and book-keepers who maintained neat entries in their small ledgers about exact amounts noted against the names of those who bet them. Vyas and his team had done this ledger work right from 13 January till the time of the raid, indicating how betting had begun right from the onset of the IPL season. For instance, Rs 9,13,600 was the account transaction entry of Master, the Pakistan bookie, with his Indian counterparts Rakesh Gangwal (Rakesh Jaipur), Devender Kothari, Ramlal Johar (Nokha), Badri Narayan Modi (Badri), Chandra Prakash Jain (Jupiter), Lambu and Lokesh.[5] Similarly, yet another Pakistani bookie code-named 'No. 70' had a total transaction with Indian bookies Lokesh, Badri, Nokha and Kothari worth Rs 4,56,900. The ledger also mentioned that Badri had already been paid Rs 3,38,900.

The police could now link Indian bookies to their Pakistan and Dubai-based counterparts. The ledgers clearly showed the details of how much money had been placed, with whom and by whom. Entries corresponding to the account of these bookies were right up to 13 May 2013, a day before the raid. The entries of that day, when the police raided Lalwani Mansion, were found on a separate sheet of paper. Right from the first day, 3 April 2013, of IPL 6 up to 13 May 2013, Vyas and his cronies had collected bets well over Rs 50 lakh – to be precise, Rs 51,55,290.

The money apart, surveillance of Vyas' mobile phone and his phone book revealed he was accepting bets from bookies in Pakistan and elsewhere. The last call he had made as a bookie was as late as 4:04 p.m. on 14 May 2013, just a few hours before the police rang the doorbell of his gambling den.

The police finally found that Vyas was using thirty SIM cards across 92 phones. Except for one SIM card bought in his associate Kadam's name, he had procured the other twenty-nine on forged documents. The police seized them all, booking him for forgery and cheating under various sections of the IPC as well as the Maharashtra Prevention of Gambling Act.

But Vyas was not the last in the chain. The arrests continued after him.

On 19 May, former Ranji player Manish Mathukarao Guddewar from Aurangabad and fixers Kiran Dhole (Munna) and Sunil Bhatia from Nagpur were arrested. Two cheques amounting to Rs 8 lakh, given by Chandila to Sunil Bhatia, and two more cheques amounting to Rs 1 lakh, along with other incriminating documents and mobile phones were recovered from this raid. Then on 21 May, Baburao Yadav was arrested from Delhi. On 24 May, Yahya (Yusuf) was arrested from Hyderabad International Airport minutes before he was set to fly to Dubai. Chandresh had got Yahya to help him in 'fixing' more players. Yahya had in fact shifted to Mumbai but, after the arrests, reached Hyderabad to escape to Dubai. On 26 May, his associates Sunil Chander Saxena (Babu) and Syed Durrey Ahmed (Shoaib) were also arrested from Hyderabad.

On 27 May, multiple raids in Delhi and the National Capital Region led to the arrest of Bhupender Nagar from Noida. It was Nagar, a security officer at a club in Delhi and also Chandila's friend, who had arranged for his meetings with fixers Nitin Jain (Susu), Vikas Chaudhary (Vicky) and Vinod Sharma (Monu) in Delhi and Jaipur to fix the matches. The police also seized Rs 50,000 that allegedly were part of Rs 5 lakh that Chandila had received from Nitin, Vikas and Vinod, who themselves had cumulatively made Rs 19 lakh out of betting, courtesy Chandila's 'delivery'. The three were arrested immediately afterwards.

The same day, Jitendra Kumar Jain, who had shared responsibility in 'fixing' Sreesanth, Ankeet, and Chandila, was also arrested from Ahmedabad. Like Baburao Yadav and Sunil Bhatia, Jitendra, too, had travelled abroad in order to 'fix' Indian and foreign players for the betting syndicate. On 29 May, Sreesanth's close friend, Abhishek Shukla, was arrested from his Mumbai flat along with the Rs 5.5 lakh that Sreesanth had received from the fixers.

As the drama rolled out, denials flew fast and furious. The one thing in common in the history of match-fixing has been the way tainted players – both Indian and overseas – react after a controversy. Back in 2000, Cronje had first rejected the charges, only later admitting to them, while every other Indian player, including Azhar, Prabhakar and Jadeja had refuted the charges. In much the same vein, all the accused players flatly denied they had been up to any wrong-doing.

But while the tainted players and others, including several BCCI officials, bore the brunt of the ire of the media and public at large, the underworld, with its fixers and bookies, was not shaken by the arrests. They knew they had maintained an arm's length with those on the field, and were nonchalant about the arrests. As per a transcript of a conversation between Salman and Firoz Farid Ansari, both D-Company associates, dated 16 May 2013 around 4:49 p.m., they took stock of the situation and wondered how deeply the police had infiltrated their syndicate. They specifically enquired about Tinku Mandi because he was one of the few people with whom they'd had direct conversation:

Salman: Hello.

Firoz: How are you?

Salman: Any news about Tinku?

Firoz: No, nothing about Tinku. The talk is only about seven people.

Salman: Who are the seven who have been arrested?

Firoz went on to list the seven who were arrested in Mumbai, which didn't include Tinku Mandi. What they didn't know was that Tinku Mandi would soon be arrested with Ajay Goyal, Amit Gupta, Dipit Garg, Ramakant Aggarwal, Deepak Kumar (Deepu) and Rakesh (Rocky). In fact, even Firoz would be arrested – nearly a month later, on 11 June – following the leads given by Vyas.

The Special Cell now had enough evidence, most of it technical and corroboratory, to nail the twenty-nine accused. They also prepared cases on ten others who were either absconding or were based in foreign lands. This process would continue over a period of a few months.

Even though some bookies were absconding, there was no doubt that this was one of the most successful investigations orchestrated by the Delhi and Mumbai Police. For Neeraj Kumar, at a professional level, it would go down as the most high-profile and rewarding case of his career, even though personally, he was left disappointed. As a lover of cricket, the murky events had left him with no faith in the sport anymore. As he famously told a newspaper soon after the police filed it first charge sheet, 'I have stopped watching IPL!'

PART II

A BRIEF HISTORY OF FIXING

10

HISTORIC CONFESSIONS

It's December 1996. South Africa, led by Hansie Cronje, is 460 runs behind India and need to survive the Indian bowling attack led by Anil Kumble. The series is locked at 1-1, and the South Africans are getting exposed on a pitch where the ball is hardly rising above their knees. But things won't exactly go South Africa's way.

The collapse begins with Gary Kirsten and Herschelle Gibbs playing down the wrong line and their team's fate is almost sealed when Daryll Cullinan takes on Captain Sachin Tendulkar's arm at mid-off, only to be run-out. South Africa goes on to register their first series defeat since losing to West Indies in April 1992. The win helps India maintain their unbeaten streak at home and is a glorious start for Sachin Tendulkar as the captain of the Indian cricket team.

Four years later, this Kanpur Test match would turn out to be the biggest controversy in the history of cricket and sully the game for years to come, just as much as the infamous 1932–33 Bodyline series affected the sport.

In April 2000, the Crime Branch of Delhi Police claimed to have stumbled upon a match-fixing scandal when they intercepted calls of a London-based businessman and suspected bookie, Sanjeev Chawla. According to them, between 8 March and 19 March 2000, Chawla and some others were conspiring to fix matches in connivance with the South African skipper Cronje. The police also claimed that Chawla was in constant touch with Cronje and had stayed in the same hotels as the teams.

Chawla had provided a phone – purchased by another accused, Rajesh Kalra – to Cronje, and the frequency of the calls between them was 'very high' at the time of the matches. The police alleged that Chawla was introduced to Cronje by Hamid 'Banjo' Cassim, a South African national, who was reported to be involved with other team members. Cassim, the police claimed, came into contact with Chawla in South Africa during the January 2000 triangular series between England, South Africa and Zimbabwe, and introduced him to Cronje. They also had information that Cronje had offered his teammate Herschelle Gibbs a hefty sum of money to score less than 20 runs in a match.

The events of 7 April 2000 would be responsible for changing the game of cricket forever. The Delhi Police charged South African Captain Hansie Cronje with fixing South Africa's ODIs against India in March. They released transcripts of an alleged conversation between Cronje and Indian businessman Rajesh Kalra, who was later arrested. The conversation was regarding the players comprising the final team, about who was 'in on the deal' and the amount to be paid to Cronje and his teammates Herschelle Gibbs, Pieter Strydom and Nicky Boje.[1]

Cronje confidently denied any involvement in the matter, and he enjoyed the support of the United Cricket Board of South Africa (UCBSA), former players and the South African media.[2] In Johannesburg, UCBSA Chief Ali Bacher defended Cronje, saying he was convinced there was no substance to the reports from India. 'Cronje is known for his unquestionable integrity and honesty,' said Bacher, adding that he had spoken to the captain immediately after he had heard the allegations from New Delhi. 'He says it is absolute rubbish. There is nothing at all in it. The UCBSA is certain that no South African cricketer has ever been involved in match-fixing.' He added that the other players had denied emphatically the allegations. Other voices joined this chorus. Coach Bob Woolmer called the allegations 'absolute garbage' and even the Christian spiritual leader pastor Ray McCauley rose to Cronje's defence and said he was 'shocked by the allegation because he knew Hansie as a person of integrity'.[3]

Cronje himself delivered the ultimate denial: 'I have been informed of the developments and I am stunned. The allegations are completely without substance. I have been privileged to play for South Africa since 1992 and I want to ensure every South African that I have made 100 per cent effort to win every match that I have played. It has been an honour to play for South Africa and I would never do anything to let my country down.'[4]

The next day, an international diplomatic crisis broke out as the South African government questioned the basis for having the players' privacy invaded by phone interceptions. India was suddenly on the back foot. Aziz Pahad, South African deputy minister of foreign affairs, assured Bacher that the government would seek an explanation for intecerption while on tour in India. The government assured that an explanation would be sought as to why the allegations against the four players were made public.

Newspaper reports claimed Cronje's innocence, and said that he had been framed. Graham Ford, South African coach, stated the Indian police had been 'overhasty' in filing the charges. 'We were never approached by any gambling syndicate. The whole story is a storm in a teacup. I am sure that when further details are made available, the innocence of Hansie and the others will be fully proved.' To make matters worse, senior cricket writer Trevor Chesterfield wrote that 'the whole thing is a hoax. I heard the alleged tape alleged between Cronje and a bookmaker being played on air. My impression is that both voices were of Asian origin. The voice that was supposed to be Hansie's did not have a South African accent. It was definitely not Hansie's voice.'

Meanwhile, the arrested Delhi businessman Rajesh Kalra admitted to offering the players $ 400,000–500,000 to fix the series. The Delhi Police also named Krishan Kumar, a failed actor and brother of T-series owner Gulshan Kumar, in the conspiracy.

Yet, Cronje continued to stand his ground, saying at a press conference with great emphasis: 'I want to make it 100 per cent clear that I deny ever receiving any sum of money during the ODI series in India. I want to also make it absolutely clear I have never spoken to any member of the team about throwing a game.'[5] Gibbs and Boje also attended the press conference and backed Cronje's story, saying neither had received any offers to fix matches. Bacher continued being offensive to Indian authorities by explaining the stand of the South African government and the UCBSA, which viewed the allegations 'in a most serious light'. He said, 'The issues at stake are the lack of protocol used on this most serious issue and the bugging of phones used by the South African team while in India.' Deputy Foreign Minister Pahad went a step further and told a Johannesburg newspaper that South Africa's High Commissioner to India had listened to excerpts from the tapes and was convinced the accents were not South African.[6]

But this concerted cover-up did not have much effect on the Indian side. In a bold move, making it very clear that they were not willing to withdraw the charges, the Delhi Police issued a statement saying they had sufficient evidence to prove Cronje was in direct contact with I Sanjay Chawla during the five ODIs played in India between 9 and 19 March 2000.

The dam finally broke. On 11 April, Cronje called up Bacher at 3 a.m. and admitted that he had been 'dishonest' about his activities in India. He acknowledged receiving $ 10,000–15,000 for 'providing information and forecast but not match-fixing' during the ODI series in India.[7]

The Delhi Police and the Indian government were finally vindicated. The UCBSA sacked Cronje with immediate effect, suspending him from the upcoming three-match ODI series against Australia. Shaun Pollock was named the new captain, and the South African government ordered a Commission of Inquiry headed by Judge Edwin King to investigate the scandal.

Cronje tried his best to extricate himself from what was fast becoming an extremely sticky wicket for him. He stated, 'While I was in India I was again contacted. I mentioned names of players, but in fact I never spoke to a single player about throwing a match. I never received any financial rewards. I wish to emphasize that the allegations of match-fixing by myself are devoid of all truth.'

As a furore broke out in the cricketing world, the South African government decided to behave like an ostrich with its head in the sand, and urged South Africans not to treat the match-fixing scandal as a 'national crisis' nor to fall into a collective depression. 'It must be dealt with by the sporting community; it is not a national political crisis at all.'[8] Newspaper polls showed that an overwhelming number of South Africans wanted Cronje to play again, even as details of the scandal began to emerge. In a poll published in *The Star*, 94 per cent of the 7,220 respondents supported Cronje playing for South Africa again. But while South Africa was desperately trying to downplay matters, world opinion was fast emerging against it.

In Durban, Denis Rogers, Chairman of the Australian Cricket Board, pushed urgently for a South African inquiry into the Cronje affair, in line with the ICC ruling. Lord MacLaurin, Chairman of the England and Wales Cricket Board, called for an urgent meeting between leading Test playing countries to discuss the controversy. 'Any player found guilty of breaching the code of conduct must be banned for life,' he stated unequivocally. Former Pakistan captain Imran Khan warned, in no uncertain terms, that the game of cricket would face further disgrace if an extensive inquiry was not launched into match fixing practices. He went on to take the opportunity to affirm that fixing was a worldwide disgrace, and not restricted to the usual suspects – India and Pakistan.

He was right to a certain extent, because until then, India's involvement with the Cronje scandal was only peripheral.

According to the Delhi Police, Krishan Kumar of T-Series had not only financed the activities of Sanjeev Chawla but had also been a partner in his dealings.[9] Krishan Kumar was eventually arrested for being one of the conduits between Rajesh Kalra and Chawla. But in typical Indian celebrity fashion, he immediately complained of angina and was hospitalized. Meanwhile, Bacher pointed out, in a desperate bid to deflect attention from South Africa, 'the game's governing body has failed to deal with match-fixing. As the latest crisis in South Africa has shown, it is a global problem. No one country can point the finger at anyone else.'[10]

On 20 April that year, Bacher was quoted as saying that two matches at the 1999 World Cup were fixed,[11] one international team was throwing and manipulating matches and an umpire was under suspicion. He was referring to the World Cup match between Pakistan and Bangladesh, which Pakistan lost. ICC Chief Jagmohan Dalmiya did not take too kindly to Bacher's declarations. 'Bacher said recently that all betting and match-fixing problems originated from the subcontinent. He took back his words within twenty-four hours. So I am now waiting for another retraction from him on the World Cup match fixing charge; otherwise, he will have to explain why he went public with his allegation.'[12] Nobody produced any concrete evidence or specific details about Bacher's allegations and no cricketing body was interested in probing this angle, so the rumours about the World Cup match being fixed were confined to drawing-room and dressing-room talks.

Meanwhile, the Delhi Police claimed to possess more than fourteen audio tapes of incriminating phone conversations that formed part of the 'clinching evidence' to nail Cronje, Gibbs, Nicky Boje and Pieter Strydom. Opener Gibbs reiterated that he was not part of any match-rigging or betting network. Gibbs told the *Cape Argus* newspaper that he was stunned when he was implicated in the fixing scandal involving Cronje. 'I felt bad but I knew I was innocent. Nothing would ever make me do something so irresponsible. Nobody approached us. When we were told about it, we were terribly shocked.'[13]

The South African team ignored all these reports and rallied in support of Cronje, with his successor Shaun Pollock declaring that the entire team was with him. Not just this, Pollock dedicated the victory against Australia in the first ODI in Durban to his predecessor.

On 8 May, T. M. Mbeki, President of South Africa, ordered the formation of a one-man judicial commission headed by Judge Edwin King to probe 'cricket match fixing and related matters'. On 7 June 2000, the King Commission began its proceedings and the pins started to fall. Former South African cricketer Pat Symcox testified that he had been approached by Cronje about 'throwing' a match against Pakistan during 1994–95. He also confirmed that in 1996, during a team meeting in Mumbai, Cronje had conveyed to the team an offer of $ 250,000 to lose a one-dayer against India.[14] On 8 June 2000, the suspended Gibbs, who had till then denied charges of match-fixing, effectively sealed Cronje's fate. He confessed he had accepted an offer from his former captain to make less than twenty runs in an ODI in India earlier in the year, in exchange of $ 15,000. Then seamer Henry Williams testified that he had been offered $ 15,000 by Cronje to bowl expensively in an ODI in India earlier in the year. Pieter Strydom revealed he had been offered money by Cronje before the first Test against India in Mumbai in February. Jacques Kallis, along with Mark Boucher and Lance Klusener, corroborated that Cronje had made an offer to the three players in a hotel room before the second Test against India at Bengaluru in March 2000.

On 11 October 2000, the UCBSA imposed a life ban on Hansie Cronje,[15] and he slipped into oblivion, taking up a job in backwater George. His name would hit headlines only two years later after he died in a cargo plane crash. In August 2006, an inquest into the plane crash was opened by South Africa's High Court, which concluded that 'the death of the deceased Cronje was brought about by an act or omission prima facie amounting to an offence on the part of pilots'. There was widespread reportage in the international media, suspecting foul play. Theories that Cronje could have been murdered because of his confessions started being openly discussed in the media.[16] There were suspicions raised about the landing controls being tampered with, which led to the crash. The reports that the betting syndicate had a hand in Cronje's death resurfaced via former Nottinghamshire coach Clive Rice in the wake of the 'accidental' death of Pakistan coach Bob Woolmer in March 2007.[17] A day after Pakistan had crashed out of the 2007 World Cup with a humiliating loss to Ireland, coach Woolmer was found unconscious in his Jamaican hotel room. He later died of a suspected heart attack.

Once again, the name of Dawood emerged from the shadows. Dawood had long been associated with the Cronje fixing scandal.

Investigators, both within South Africa and beyond, believed they had enough indications of his involvement when the fixers approached Cronje for the first time.[18] But there was no concrete evidence of the linkage. There were no phone recordings to support the suspicion either. There were only reports that Dawood had shifted base from Dubai to London, and was constantly shuttling between the two cities during the time Cronje was lured into fixing.

Cronje had always claimed he did not even know the man called John who had first approached him to throw an ODI against Pakistan in the Mandela Cup in Cape Town in January 1995 for $ 10,000; he was unsure whether the man originated from India or Pakistan.

Now, as the murder theories emerged, investigators, both Indian and African, were aware that the underworld, headed by Dawood, would not hesitate to eliminate one former cricketer, who was at the time just an accounts manager in a firm that manufactured construction equipment.

On 12 October 2006, the Delhi Police finally managed to question Gibbs for over two hours about the South African tour of India in 2000. Gibbs had allegedly named Derek Crookes, the former South African spinner, as being involved in match-fixing, and had denied his own role.[19] The next day, Crookes of course, expressed shock at being linked to the fixing allegations, saying he had been cleared by the King Commission.

On 11 December 2007, the Delhi Police managed to question Nicky Boje, who had come over to play in the Indian Cricket League. This was the first time he was coming to India after the scandal broke in 2000. He had skipped the two-Test tour of India in November 2004, fearing action by the Indian police. However, he, too, denied any role in fixing matches.

So, the only star player who admitted to fixing matches in the first-ever scandal that broke out in the cricketing world, that too in India, was a dead man called Hansie Cronje!

11

FALLOUT IN INDIA AND ELSEWHERE

While Hansie Cronje's confession began to create shockwaves across the cricketing world, the Indian camp was divided. Allegations were being hurled from various quarters of the cricketing fraternity, and the strong wall of unity shared by the cricketers had started to crumble. While former captains Sunil Gavaskar and Dilip Vengsarkar took a strong stand against match fixing cricketers, saying, 'if found guilty, none should be spared, past or present,' BCCI Secretary Jaywant Lele dismissed the allegations as 'rubbish', saying, 'As far as we are concerned, there is nothing. Everything is okay.'[1]

The first stone was thrown by South African newspaper *The Star* on 13 April 2000. It reported that the mysterious South African go-between, Hamid 'Banjo' Cassim, a Johannesburg businessman and friend of Cronje, was linked to Indian cricketers

Mohammad Azharuddin and Sachin Tendulkar, who immediately denied any links with Cassim. But Azhar admitted to knowing him, as did other Indian players. 'He used to bring Indian food for us in South Africa. But that does not mean I have any links with him.' Tendulkar repeated the same: 'He got us Indian food, especially vegetarian. That's all that my relationship with him was.'

A shadow had been cast on Indian cricket. Former BCCI president I. S. Bindra used this opportunity to press home his allegation that the BCCI had hushed up information about three Indian Test players who were betting against their own team. 'Between 1996 and 2000, the BCCI was told repeatedly that three players were indulging in betting, but it glossed the matter over. Two tour managers and one coach had also mentioned in their reports that some players were taking part in unlawful activities. Every BCCI member knows the identity of the players. It is no secret.'[2] On CNN, he named Manoj Prabhakar as one of the players, and went on to add that Prabhakar had named former captain Kapil Dev as being involved in this unlawful activity.

Former BCCI president Raj Singh Dungarpur denied this outright. He said, 'No action was taken because no such incidents were reported during my tenure from 1996 to 1999.' But the government had been forced to intervene, especially in light of the Cronje affair. It asked the BCCI for a report on the recent poor performances of the Indian team, with then sports minister, Sukhdev Singh Dhindsa, stating he could not rule out match fixing as a cause for them. A prominent list of people petitioned for the involvement of the CBI in the investigation, with former Indian captains Mansoor Ali Khan Pataudi and Bishen Singh Bedi in favour, as were the Opposition parties. The Congress demanded an investigation into charges of foreign exchange violations and criminal links between bookies and drug barons, saying that a CBI probe was essential since the scandal had global implications.

The BCCI responded by saying it would welcome other investigative agencies, but the findings of the Chandrachud Committee on match-fixing would be discussed in Parliament and made public. As a defensive move, it also decided to implement a six-point code of conduct for players, broadly based on suggestions made by the ICC Code of Conduct Commission, headed by Lord Hugh Griffith.

But Bindra was not mollified by these half measures. He continued to make shocking allegations against the players without naming any of them, and claimed that 'cheating is rampant in international cricket.'[3] He even went so far as to call Hansie Cronje a 'hero' whose confession would save the game. 'Virtually every match in international cricket is fixed in one form or another. Match-fixing is as old as the game itself,' he told reporters in New Delhi. 'Hansie is a small fish. There are still many sharks out there.'

The BCCI fought this onslaught by claiming lack of evidence. As A.C. Muthiah put it, 'If he [Bindra] has evidence, he must hand it over to the police.' But it was fighting a losing battle. The then Indian coach Kapil Dev chipped in with his own suspicions, saying, 'I no longer have any doubt that something is going on.'[4]

As the country erupted in outrage, the Vajpayee government pledged the full force of law to investigate the match-fixing allegations even as it released the three-year-old Chandrachud Committee report that gave a clean chit to Indian players. 'The government shall leave no stone unturned to get to the bottom of any charges, whether through a probe by the CBI or any other investigative agency,' Sports Minister S. S. Dhindsa told the Parliament.[5]

But Bindra was not one to remain silent. He claimed that after his allegations, he had got calls saying his children's lives were under threat. 'Both my wife and I received phone calls threatening us about our children's lives,'[6] he said, adding that the fixing racket was led by a handful of cricket administrators in tandem with certain vested commercial interests. He then threw an open challenge at ICC Chief Jagmohan Dalmiya, inviting him for a public debate. 'The ICC Chief should have replied to my charges regarding betting, match-fixing, manipulation of players and the privatization of cricket in the garb of globalization.'

The government had had enough. Union Home Minister L. K. Advani declared a 'comprehensive' inquiry led by the CBI into the match fixing charges.[7]

●

As accusations of match fixing flew fast and wide, former Indian skipper Mohammad Azharuddin's name began to be mentioned in all the unexpected and wrong places. A *Gulf News* report stated that a leading Pakistani jeweller in Dubai had gifted Azharuddin, then captain, a Mercedes Benz car during a lucky draw he had conducted on behalf of his firm to celebrate India's win during the Coca Cola Cricket Cup in November 1998.[8] When *Outlook* magazine reported it, Azhar reacted by saying the editor should have known that a car, unlike a toy, could not be brought into India without government and public knowledge.[9]

Interestingly though, what has never been brought on record and hence remains unsubstantiated is the claim by some of the investigators that the businessman who gifted the Mercedes to Azhar was none other than Dawood Ibrahim himself! But this piece of news got overlooked as the battle over Cronje continued. On 15 June 2000, Cronje came up with a shocker: he told the King Commission that Azharuddin had introduced him to a bookie who offered him money to throw a 1996 Test match during South Africa's tour of India.

Cronje told the commission that Azharuddin introduced him to one Mukesh Gupta – known in betting circles as MK – from whom he received $ 30,000 in return for a promise to throw the third Test match at Kanpur – the aforementioned game at the beginning of the previous chapter. In his long-awaited testimony, Cronje dwelt almost entirely on the temptations and perils he had met in the subcontinent as well as in encounters with players from the subcontinent. The other international cricketer he named was Pakistan's Salim Malik.

Cronje admitted at the very outset that he had lied repeatedly, saying he did this to protect the younger players. He admitted his initial public denials to the UCBSA were untruthful. He went on to depose that the letter of 11 April 2000 was also untruthful in a number of respects, as were the subsequent press statements issued on his instructions. He had misled the UCBSA and members of the South African government, and had also withheld facts from his legal representatives. He categorically stated he had not been honest and hence apologized unreservedly.

In his twenty-three-page testimony, Cronje said his very first exposure to the world of betting and match-fixing was during an ODI against Pakistan in the Mandela Cup at Cape Town in January 1995, when 'an Indian or Pakistani who introduced himself only as John' offered him about $ 10,000 for the team to throw the game. The second time was 'at some stage during the 1996 Indian tour,' when he was approached by one 'Sunil' who asked him if he was interested in fixing matches, to which he replied in the negative. But it was through Azhar, he said, that he entered into something that he had been avoiding all along:

'On the evening of the third day of the third Test against India at Kanpur, I received a call from Mohammad Azharuddin, who was friendly with a number of South African players. He called me to a room in the hotel and introduced me to Mukesh Gupta (MK). Azharuddin then left us alone . . . MK asked me if we would give wickets away on the last day of that Test to ensure that we lost. He asked me to speak to the other players, and gave me approximately $ 30,000 in cash to do so. I led him to believe that I would.

This seemed an easy way to make money, but I had no intention of doing anything. I did not speak to any other player and did nothing to influence the match. In the event, however, we lost the Test. I had effectively received money for doing nothing and I rationalized that this was somehow acceptable because I had not actually done anything.[10]

MK, however, made another offer during the tour, Cronje said, when his team was offered $ 200,000 to throw the last ODI of the tour. Cronje was asked to convey the offer to the team, which he consented to. By that stage of the 'long and arduous tour', Cronje said, the team was exhausted and a number of key players were suffering from injuries. Explaining that he could not recall the exact sequence of events which took place 'a long time ago', Cronje said he spoke about the offer to some players beforehand and later at a team meeting on the eve of the match 'attended by all the players in the squad'. The team, however, rejected the offer, with Andrew Hudson, Daryll Cullinan and Derek Crookes speaking out strongly against it. Despite this, a few players stayed back after the meeting and 'we chatted about the matter'. Curious to see whether the offer could be increased, Cronje says he telephoned MK and asked to increase the amount to $ 300,000. 'MK said this was too much but was ready to pay $ 250,000. This new offer was discussed the next morning before the match and rejected.'

All in all, Cronje confessed to taking about $ 100,000 in bribes from gamblers since 1996, but he claimed he had never thrown or fixed a match. He also announced his retirement from cricket, concluding that his 'great passion for the game and for my teammates' was matched by 'an unfortunate love for money' – famous words that sealed his fate.

●

There may have been similarities in the modus operandi adopted in the 2000 and 2013 fixing scandals – for example, much like Chawla did in 2000, the bookies of 2013 had also bought Sreesanth and Chandila smart BlackBerry phones and designer glasses – but the events and the outcomes of 2000 and 2013 were different in a couple of ways.

Expensive consumer and lifestyle goods were traded in for pure cash in 2013. Moreover, back in 2000, cricketers faced allegations about their proximity with bookies and gangsters during parties and social events, but there were no allegations of direct involvement of players negotiating with the bookies. And despite the reality of the 2010 spot-fixing scandal, when some Pakistani players were banned for life, Sreesanth, Chandila and Ankeet thought nothing of hobnobbing with the bookies and the underworld.

In 2013, one could say the situation even worsened, as Chhota Shakeel threatened players in order to recover the betting money. The players continued to indulge in spot-fixing, knowing very well that the bookies were hand in gloves with the underworld and that they were 'doing' the matches for major financial gains, entirely dependent on fixed moments of the match. The whole fixing game seemed to have reached a new level in 2013 and many suspect that the real story is even bigger.

This supposed truth is often stated in hushed tones amongst police officials and giggled away by fixers who are still at large and continuing their 'work'. There is a strong suspicion that match-fixing today involves not just cricketers, underworld elements or even some failed film personalities, but also has its fair share of people from politics and sports associations. Consequently, one is tempted to believe that when the police arrest a few cricketers, that's about as far as it will go, as the investigation will never get beyond basic questioning of a few film personalities, bookies and cricketers. The probe then hits a dead end.

The cost of the probe is perhaps too heavy to pay for whoever supports this from the political sphere. Perhaps, the police know who this 'whoever' is, but they are not willing to even whisper about it. Perhaps that is why the fixer interviewed for this book said: '*Bacche faltu mein fasgaye*! (The boys were arrested for nothing!)' Perhaps, that is also why, when the Delhi Police filed a 90-page charge sheet on 22 July 2013, more than thirten years after match-fixing firs broke out, the only cricketer to be named in the charge sheet was a dead Hansie Cronjie; the charge sheet named Kishan Kumar, Rajesh Kalra and Sunil Dara (Bittoo) as the accused, while asking the court for the extradition of the other two accused – Sanjeev Chawla, who is reportedly in the UK, and Manmohan Khattar, who is in the US.

12

THE FALL OF AZHAR

Mohammad Azharuddin, born 8 February 1963, was hailed by many as a 'magician on the field', his willow compared to a wand, with strokes that could cast a spell. But even without the lyrical magic of his batting, statistically, he remains one of India's most successful captains, winning 103 ODIs, an Indian record. His record of fourteen Test wins as captain was broken and bettered by his successor Sourav Ganguly with twenty-one Test match wins. After having worn the badge of honour as the national team captain far longer than any other cricketer till then, Azharuddin's career came to a grinding halt in light of the Cronje affair.

On 15 June 2000, Hansie Cronje claimed that Azharuddin had introduced him to bookie MK in 1996. India hoped and prayed that Cronje was lying. They didn't want to believe their cricketing god would have feet of clay. But alas! Azhar's wicket fell in 2000, when the CBI confirmed his participation in fixing matches during the South African tour of India.[1] Almost overnight, his batting magic gave way to the dark arts and he was awarded a lifetime ban by the BCCI.

According to investigation reports, the story of Azhar's downfall began with a small punter from Delhi called Anand Saxena way back in 1986.

Anand Saxena was a Delhi punter, betting not just on cricket but also on tennis, football and hockey. By 1986, he had made a small fortune and reached Bombay to start placing bets with the biggest bookies of that time, Mama and Kamate, whose reference had been given to him by one R. P. Singh, a veteran on the betting field in Delhi.

In 1988, he went to watch the Ram Charan Aggarwal Tournament being played in Delhi between different clubs. There he saw cricketer Ajay Sharma playing in a particular match on which he made a few quick bucks. After that match, he met with Sharma and paid him Rs 2,000 as a token of his appreciation, and told him that if he ran into any problem in life, he could contact him or his partner MK. Saxena did this simply because he thought Sharma had talent, and it was a smart investment done in the hope that he could reap the benefits someday.

Sure enough, after about fifteen days, Sharma got in touch with him and the two began a mutually beneficial relationship, possibly the first recorded instance of a punter–player nexus in its simplest format.

Saxena became partners with Delhi bookie Mukesh Gupta, also known as MK or John, in 1987. In 1990, when India was touring New Zealand and both Ajay Sharma and Manoj Prabhakar were in the team, MK requested Sharma over a call to introduce him to Prabhakar. It's interesting to learn that while MK was introduced to Prabhakar by Ajay Sharma, Saxena already knew Prabhakar through his wife who ran a beauty parlour, which Manoj Prabhakar's wife often visited. Later, when Saxena was questioned on whether he was in touch with Prabhakar during the latter's association with MK, he stated that MK was secretive about his links with cricketers – an indication that the partnership between MK and Saxena was already breaking up and MK was making his own inroads into the cricketing world.

During the New Zealand tour, MK regularly spoke to Sharma to gain information about the weather, pitch, team composition, etc., and made profits in his business. After the tour, however, Sharma was dropped from the team touring England. Now, Prabhakar became MK's 'informant', and was paid a sum of Rs 40,000 to help him during the tour. MK also promised to pay him money equivalent to that of a Maruti Gypsy's price for the information. According to him, Prabhakar not only gave him information about all aspects of the Indian team, but also underperformed in one of the Test matches which ended in a draw. After the tour, when the team returned to India, MK fulfilled his promise and paid money to Prabhakar to get his dream car – a Gypsy with wide tyres!

The investment in Prabhakar proved to be sound and opened many doors for MK. Around that time, MK visited Prabhakar's house in Ghaziabad for a dinner, where Prabhakar promised to introduce him to other international players, pegging the charge of introduction at Rs 50,000 per player. After dinner that night, he immediately spoke to Gus Logie of West Indies over the phone. However, Logie refused to cooperate. Sometime thereafter, the Sri Lankan team visited India, and Prabhakar introduced Aravinda de Silva to MK for a price. MK established a good rapport with de Silva and later contacted him for an introduction to Martin Crowe of New Zealand, whom he met in 1991 in New Zealand and paid him a sum of $ 20,000 in exchange for information. MK also met Salim Malik and paid him Rs 8 lakh to fix a match between the ultimate Indian winners of the Wills Trophy and the Pakistan team without the knowledge of Javed Miandad. In Sri Lanka, where the Indian team was participating in some friendly matches, Prabhakar introduced MK to Dean Jones, for which Prabhakar received a hefty brokerage of Rs 2 lakh. MK offered an amount of $ 40,000 to Jones in exchange of information about the Australian team's strategy, morale, composition, probable result, etc., whenever they played. Jones promised to think about the offer, but backed out fearing his career would be jeopardized.

In the course of its investigation, the CBI would recast MK's use of the word 'information'. They found it difficult to believe that in an age where television had brought cricket to the drawing room with expert commentators thoroughly analyzing various aspects of the match, the information provided by a player would be of much use to a bookie. They concluded that the word 'information' was a euphemism for underperforming or 'fixing'.

For example, in a Ranji Trophy quarter-final match between Delhi and Bombay in 1991, Prabhakar had informed MK that some Delhi players were scheduled to play league cricket in England on a certain date that clashed with future Ranji matches, and hence they had decided to lose this match. The Delhi side comprised Kirti Azad, Maninder Singh, Atul Wassan, K. P. Bhaskar, Ajay Sharma, Bantoo Singh, and Prabhakar among others. MK paid Prabhakar for this information and, sure enough, Delhi lost that match as Bombay scored one more run in the first innings.

In 1992, MK struck a deal with Prabhakar to fix some of the matches in the upcoming series against Australia just prior to the World Cup. Prabhakar allegedly claimed that Navjot Singh Sidhu was with him in this deal. In fact, according to MK, Sidhu was part of nearly all of Prabhakar's fixes. Ajay Sharma corroborated this by stating Sidhu had once shown him a bag containing a large amount of money that he was going to pass off as 'farm income'. But the CBI couldn't press charges against him as they didn't have any more evidence.

However, on CNN's Q&A programme, Bindra, of BCCI, revealed that Prabhakar had told him that Kapil Dev had once come to his room during the 1994 Singer Cup in Colombo while he was in the bathroom, and his roommate Sidhu had called out saying *Paaji* had come with an offer. Kapil Dev allegedly offered him Rs 25 lakh to underperform in the next match against Pakistan. All hell broke loose when the story came out in the media, and Kapil Dev vehemently denied any of it. The only 'eyewitness' to this alleged incident, Sidhu, stated no such incident had taken place in his presence.

Former India fast bowler Prashant Vaidya was in the room adjoining 'the scene of the crime', and Prabhakar, desperately searching for support, turned to him, confident that due to his room's close proximity, he would be able to corroborate Kapil Dev had indeed offered him Rs 25 lakh to underperform in that fateful ODI. Vaidya, keen to stay out of the mess, pleaded ignorance. The only conclusive effect from this episode was the bad blood between a one-time exclusive group of legends. But it was clear that the battle lines had been drawn, with allegations flying thick and fast.

Prabhakar was boxed into a corner by now, and hard-pressed to provide evidence of some kind. For every allegation, there was a denial and a counter question: 'What proof do you have?' But no proof was forthcoming. The CBI did their best to check Kapil Dev's personal records, but no evidence of contact with known brokers came to light, so no charges could be pressed against him.

In an interview with Karan Thapar on the BBC, Kapil Dev famously broke down when asked about the allegations of match-fixing against him. He said, 'I will commit suicide than take a bribe.' The interview made headlines for all the wrong reasons, with a section of the media rallying around the 'fallen icon' and questioning Prabhakar's motives. A rival section praised Prabhakar for his forthright attitude, asking if Kapil Dev's crying was a carefully managed stunt.

But the show went on, and nothing much came out of Prabhakar's allegations. However, MK continued to sing, and his dealings with other cricketers went on across various matches, courtesy of Prabhakar's efforts. He baited Mark Waugh for $ 20,000, Alec Stewart for £ 5000, Brian Lara for $ 40,000 and Aravinda de Silva finally agreed to underperform in a Test at Lucknow for $ 15,000. But MK's own relationship with Prabhakar was approaching a dead end. MK believed Prabhakar had become very money-minded, and had gotten involved with other bookies from Delhi and Mumbai, and even with some big punters. He began to wonder about Prabhakar's loyalty, and doubted his information. As he feared, most of his information started turning out to be incorrect, beginning with the 1992 World Cup, during which MK lost a lot of money. Then Prabhakar's incessant demands for monies more than what he deserved angered MK, who discontinued his association with both Prabhakar and Saxena.

During this time, Ajay Sharma resurfaced in MK's life and asked him for Rs 15,000 to help him purchase a Maruti Zen car, as he was running short of money. This meeting proved to be providential. During this meeting, Sharma promised him an introduction to Azharuddin himself. MK was ecstatic. Keeping his promise, Sharma fixed a meeting with Azhar at Taj Palace Hotel, Delhi, sometime in 1995, and was paid Rs 5 lakh for his effort. The deal with Azhar fell in place earlier than expected. Azharuddin wanted somebody to finance a 'fashion show' and some 'charity matches'; in addition, MK was to pay him Rs 1.25 crore. While Azhar would deny being part of any such deal, Ajay Sharma in his statement recorded that Azharuddin had confirmed to him over phone that he had received Rs 50 lakh from MK as an advance with the arrangement that the initial amount would be adjusted against the matches he would 'do' for MK.

When the Titan Cup came up in 1996, MK wanted Azharuddin to fix some matches. Azhar agreed and allegedly took the help of Ajay Jadeja and Nayan Mongia to pull it off. Dr Ali Irani, physiologist to the Indian team (1987–97), who acted as a conduit between Azharuddin and the betting syndicate, had also stated that he had absolutely no doubt about the involvement of Jadeja with Azharuddin. But the Titan Cup final did not turn out as planned. After this disappointment, MK, along with Ajay Sharma, went to Hyderabad and met Azharuddin to ask him to compensate for the 'losses' suffered by him during the tournament. Azharuddin agreed to compensate him in future matches, and he delivered on his promise by giving MK 'information' about two Tests at Ahmedabad and Calcutta in the 1996 series against South Africa, which helped him partially recover his losses.

According to Azhar, he helped MK only with the Titan Cup and a match in the 1997 Pepsi Asia Cup.[2] But the CBI believed that his admission of having helped fix only two matches for MK was a dilution of the facts in the context of the money he had received from MK. This contention was supported by Dr Irani, who said he received a commission of Rs 25,000–50,000 from Azharuddin for receiving payments on his behalf, which ran into a couple of lakh on each occasion.[3]

But this was not the only time Ajay Sharma brought a fixer to Azhar. As his association with MK ended sometime in 1996–97, he began to move around with a certain Ajay Gupta, who was well-known punter of Delhi along with his cousins Nishit Goel, Gyan Gupta and his son Ameesh Gupta. Ajay Sharma introduced Azharuddin to Ajay Gupta and the others sometime in 1998 at the same Taj Palace in Delhi, along with Sanjay Anand, a member of Roshanara Club, a mutual friend of both Ajay Sharma and the Guptas. Ajay Sharma and Sanjay Anand received Rs 5 lakh each from the Guptas for this introduction.

Azharuddin at first refuted this accusation saying he had met Ajay Gupta to seek his help in getting a petrol pump allotted to him at Bengaluru, but later admitted that Ajay Gupta had approached him to 'fix' matches.[4] Azhar claimed he had helped fix only one match, the 1999 Pepsi Cup match between India and Pakistan at Jaipur, for the Guptas, after which he received around Rs 10 lakh from an 'unknown' person on behalf of the Guptas. Ajay Sharma, however, contradicted this claim by stating he had collected Rs 15 lakh from Ajay Gupta on Azharuddin's behalf and had deposited the money in Azharuddin's locker at Hotel Taj Palace through the then Food and Beverage manager, Anil Saxena, who used to handle Azharuddin's locker in his absence.[5]

As cell phone records would later reveal, call frequencies between the Guptas and Azhar would peak during the 'fixed' match days. One match in point was the last day of the India–South Africa Test at Bangalore. Azharuddin made a call on 6 March 2000 to Ajay Gupta. Similarly, he called Gupta on 19 March 2000 on the day of the India–South Africa ODI at Nagpur.[6]

Azhar was taken care of by the Gupta clan, with Ameesh Gupta paying for his shopping at Harrods, London, during the 1999 World Cup, and settling his five-star hotel bills in Delhi. In turn, the CBI believed that Azhar fixed several matches for them in view of the large sums of money he received and the 'hospitality' he enjoyed through them. But Azhar stuck to his guns, saying he had helped fix only one match. Then, in a desperate bid for some shades of white to his fast blackening name, he claimed that gangster Abu Salem had rung him up on a couple of occasions threatening him with dire consequences if he refused to fix certain matches. However, he 'bravely' refused to do it.

Sadly, India was in no mood to sympathize with him. When all else seemed to fail, Azhar protested he was being targeted because he belonged to a certain community and not because he had done anything wrong. The BCCI banned him in 2000, but lifted its ban in 2006, stating that other countries had not come down on their players so hard. As if that was not enough, they even honoured him, along with other Indian Test captains, at a ceremony in Mumbai during the 2006 ICC Champions Trophy. Then on 8 November 2012, the Andhra Pradesh high court lifted the life ban on Azharuddin, saying the ban was 'unsustainable'. He formally joined the Indian National Congress party on 19 February 2009, contesting the 2009 General Elections from Moradabad in western Uttar Pradesh. He won by a margin of more than 50,000 votes over his nearest rival, Kunwar Sarvesh Kumar Singh of the BJP.

However, despite his achievements, history will continue to remember Azhar not as the great batsman who made Indian cricket reach new heights, but as the batsman and captain who sold his team for a few good clothes and shoes.

13

THE ONES WHO GOT AWAY

The Azhar saga seemed to present the worst sort of a farce to the Indian cricket fan. Despite being embroiled in the controversy and allegations into fixing matches, and a life ban on participating in the sport, he turned from a law breaker to a law maker. Azhar has done it all – the reckless spending courtesy of the bookies, the expensive gifts of Rolexes and real estate to his then starlet girlfriend Sangeeta Bijlani, the wheeling and dealing with politicians, and finally finding solace in politics. One would have hoped that his sordid affair on both sides of the cricket field would be a lesson for future generation of cricketers, but unfortunately, it seemed to have had a reverse effect on our players!

The flaw at the time perhaps lay in the method of collecting the evidence. In order to build its case, the CBI essentially relied upon admissions of guilt made by Azharuddin and Ajay Sharma. These two were, by all accounts, forced to discard their early claims of innocence because of the testimony provided by a group of bookmakers. The basis for the CBI's conclusions at the time was constituted by the testimony recorded from nineteen luminaries of the betting business – variously described as bookmakers and punters. This had, in turn, been matched with the evidence given by fourteen cricketers and five officials associated with the game through the 1990s. Supplementary information was provided by telephone records, principally of cell phone calls made by principal suspects, which testified to their close interactions at critical moments in the execution of the match-fixing stratagems.

Match-fixing by its very nature is extremely devious, thus rendering it difficult for an investigation to make any headway without the cooperation of all the actors. The experience of the CBI in this respect has not been any different. They recorded how at every stage in their inquiry, they had to face a 'conspiracy of silence' from the cricketing fraternity, which included both players past and present as well as officials. It took the CBI much labour to assemble various shreds of evidence into a coherent body of information that could then be used to confront the recalcitrant witnesses. At different stages in this process of attrition, the CBI recorded that some of the players and bookmakers 'broke down and disclosed their involvement in the malpractices in various degrees'.

For all its efforts, it is probable that the CBI had only partially uncovered the dimensions of the cricket racket. Since it had to rely, almost exclusively, on the confessions of the accused, the strategy of obdurate denial could have obscured much wrong doing. This approach stood in marked contrast to that adopted by Justice Mallik Abdul Qayyum in Pakistan.

Confronted with the same conundrum, Justice Qayyum adopted an analytical approach of his own, studying the course of various matches and their outcomes, and corelating them with the performances of key players under suspicion.

CBI sleuths failed to come up with convincing answers as to exactly how the players could be tried in court, no matter how damning the evidence. The only provision that could be applied was the notorious section 420 of the Indian Penal Code, which was used in cases of cheating and fraud. But who had the cricketers defrauded? And how could it be proved that giving information about the condition of the pitch was cheating?

At the time, the best the CBI could do was go after Azharuddin and Sharma, both of whom were employed by the government-owned State Bank of India though being cricketers in the Indian Team, and thus could be prosecuted as public servants and tried under the Prevention of Criminal Act. But it wasn't done. The CBI, for some reason, hadn't been as aggressive in pinning down the criminals. In fact, the Andhra Pradesh High Court also pointed out that the CBI report was not 'comprehensive' and it did not have proper evidence against Azhar.

Why did the CBI not present a robust case against the 2000 match fixing scam? Was it really true, as Neeraj Kumar had stated, that there was 'pressure from the top' to not investigate further? Why, even after eighteen years of the scam, have the photographs and phone records not become part of the evidence? Why was the one and only statement on match-fixing, made by none other than

Sachin Tendulkar, never highlighted in the media? At the time, Tendulkar had said that he too believed Azhar did not give his 100 per cent.[1] Is it an unspoken contract that two MPs cannot speak ill of each other? Is that why, on Sachin's recent retirement, Azhar went out of his way to term Gavaskar and Sachin as the greatest cricketers of India? Finally, in 2012, barely four hours after its working committee failed to reach a consensus on Azharuddin, the BCCI surprised one and all by inviting the tainted former skipper to its annual awards function, at which cricketing legend Sunil Gavaskar was given a lifetime achievement award.

Even the ICC frowned upon the way BCCI handled Azhar. Sharad Pawar, then BCCI president, echoed the views of his predecessor and Punjab Cricket Association Chief, I. S. Bindra, who had said the ICC was following double standards when it came to dealing with players accused of match fixing from India and those from other countries. 'There are other countries fielding tainted players like (Herschelle) Gibbs and (Shane) Warne. We are not playing him (Azharuddin). He is not going to play any more.'[2] Pawar said, in a lame justification for not coming down harder on Azhar, knowing very well that at 37, Azhar anyway couldn't have played for much longer. Once he was officially acquitted, BCCI felicitated him for his 'contribution' to Indian cricket as a captain. The award function was well attended by cricketers and political administrators.

And what happened to the other accused? From being the accuser, tables were turned on Manoj Prabhakar, and the former Delhi and India all-rounder was now the accused; not just the accused, but pronounced guilty as well. But had justice been doled out? Not really. What about Sidhu and Kapil Dev? Reinventing himself as India's comedy king, Sidhu went on to make a fortune for himself, and Kapil Dev was honoured with the C. K. Nayudu Lifetime Achievement Award by the BCCI at its Seventh Annual Awards Ceremony in January 2014. Even though Kapil and Sidhu were never in the same league as Azhar and Prabhakar and weren't ever accused, can we ever be sure they truly didn't know what was going on? Staying silent about a crime is the same as complicity.

At this moment, it makes no difference whether you are a fan of Kapil Dev or Prabhakar. It hardly matters which side of the story you believe. Looking back eighteen years later, all of them are still making money out of their cricketing association. Today in 2019, Azhar, Prabhakar and Kapil Dev all hog the limelight during prime-time discussions on cricket, and perhaps earn more than they would have as players.

The subplot of the Indian fallout on Cronje's confession has completely lost its steam after 18 long years of cricket of all kinds – Test, ODI, T20. People who had been accused in the scam went on to become commentators, columnists, experts – most of them went back into the cricket business. Who knows, if the winds of politics sway his way, Azhar could even be made sports minister in the future? Incidentally, as an interesting contrast, Cronje was barred from South Africa's Sports Hall of Fame.

The truly sad part about the 2000 scam was that not only the cricketers, but the bookies also emerged unscathed. In January 2014, even as the IPL spot-fixing case continued to intrigue the cops, they stumbled upon a huge cash reserve amounting to Rs 15–20 crore as part of pay-offs meant for bettors. The money was being taken to an undisclosed destination after a robbery in Delhi. And barely six months after the IPL scam broke out, bookie Rajesh Kalra confessed that the entire amount was *hawala* money that was supposed to be returned to an unknown source.

Kalra had close links with other bookies and was active in betting circles. He also had close links with Chandresh Jain and Sanjeev Chawla. What was interesting was that Kalra's name had reappeared after fourteen years! The same Kalra had figured in the charge sheet filed by the Delhi Police in the Hansie Cronje saga. And he had resurfaced in the IPL scam as well. From 2000 to 2014, Kalra and thousands of bookies like him continued with their trade, and the law was unable to make them close shop.

It's entirely possible that even after the Mudgal Committee drama subsides, the accusations will be forgotten and the evidence lost; Sreesanth and company may very well escape the net and carry on with their lives, maybe even become ministers. Some voices may want to shout in outrage against the futility of the law, but history will teach them to save their breath and turn on their TVs instead and sit down to enjoy another fixed match.

PART III

THOSE WHO PULL THE STRINGS

14

THE VINDOO–ASAD NEXUS

By now, we are aware that some of the most dangerous criminals in the world pull the strings and control the game of cricket in India. If we were to attempt a defence of the gangsters and their actions in match-fixing, we could argue it may actually be an improvement in their trade. At least, they're not making money through murder anymore. Cheating and fraud, after all, are the core activities of the underworld, so why be outraged when they are doing exactly what is expected of them?

The question becomes interesting only when you wonder if people you least expect it from were to do it – people with power, influence and authority. People who are respected and come from the educated class of India, belonging to some of the most prominent families. But is the same act done by the 'good guys' more reprehensible than that done by the 'bad guys'?

Vindoo Dara Singh's role in the story of the IPL 2013 scam would prove to be important not only for his own involvement in betting, but also because of two other linked events: bringing to light the names of those who were supposed to be beyond reproach, people entrusted with keeping the sport above board – the first, Asad Rauf, an umpire, and the second, Gurunath Meiyappan, a Team Principal who was the son-in-law of the chairman of the governing body of cricket in all of India!

●

If Kishen Kumar was the poster boy for B-grade celebrity involvement in match fixing in 2000, it was Vindoo Dara Singh, a failed actor and son of late Dara Singh, Bollywood's much-acclaimed and celebrated wrestler–actor, who became the face of the 2013 IPL scam. For this, credit needs to be given to the interrogation of bookie Ramesh Vyas, whose phone calls revealed his links with Virender Dara Singh Randhava, popularly known as Vindoo in tinsel-town circles.

The Mumbai Crime Branch had put Vindoo's phone under surveillance since the first week of April and through almost the entire IPL season. On 20 May 2013, even after the first arrests had been made in the IPL scam, the police noticed that Vindoo was placing bets with bookie Sandeep Chhabra (Pawan Jaipur). He was doing so with two mobile phone connections, one of which was registered in the name of his driver Mahesh Mishra.

In an overnight raid on Vindoo's Juhu residence on 20 May 2013, the police recovered three cell phones allegedly belonging to bookies Sanjay Jaipur and Pawan Jaipur. The police had information that Vindoo had helped them flee India after giving them accommodation at a five-star hotel in Juhu on 14 May; he had personally driven them to the airport the following day when they caught a flight to Dubai.

What tumbled out of Vindoo's Juhu house were more than his laptop, iPad and a few mobile phones. The police learnt that Vindoo was himself a bookie who went by the code name of Jack! He was found taking bets on the phone and passing some of them to bigger bookies like Jupiter, Tinku, Sanjay Jaipur and Pawan Jaipur. On 21 May 2013, the Mumbai Crime Branch arrested him on charges of betting and aiding the bookies.

The 49-year-old Vindoo was not a familiar name with the Indian masses or even film aficionados. His only imprint in recent public memory till then was his victory at Bigg Boss Season 3, the reality show, in December 2009. But his minor celebrity status had been enough to open doors for him, that of cricketers in particular. For instance, he was close to M. S. Dhoni's wife Sakshi Dhoni and was seen sitting next to her at several IPL matches, including the 6 April 2013 one between Mumbai Indians and Chennai Super Kings. These pictures would later ignite further suspicion in the eyes of the law.

Vindoo's minor celebrity status was derived from his father. Dara Singh symbolized the collective consciousness of the Indian middle class. Everybody adored him, from the young to the old; many had read about his famous wrestling bouts with the great King Kong, and kids knew him as the Hanuman of Ramanand Sagar's *Ramayana*. His acting prowess was almost never questioned. In fact, in his later years, it did not even matter whether he crushed villains or not; Dara Singh's mere presence in any given film generated awe among the audiences. He was 'Rustam-e-Hind' (Champion of India) after all. In 2003, he became the first sportsperson to be nominated to the Rajya Sabha.

It was difficult for the public to stomach that the son of their adorable, larger-than-life star was being accused of gambling and betting on cricket matches, but the evidence was all too clear to be questioned. The transcripts of conversations between Vindoo and bookie Pawan Jaipur painted an all-too-clear picture of the various activities and transactions taking place in the bookie and betting circles.

The first big name that came into the police net as a result of these conversations was Gurunath Meiyappan, the son-in-law of BCCI supremo N. Srinivasan. Gurunath would place bets through Vindoo, sometimes even during the course of an IPL match, as became evident from the transcripts produced by the Mumbai Police.[1]

The telephonic and betting contacts with the bookies and punters were not the only things that Vindoo had to his credit. He had done what no other fixer had done in that season. Instead of going to the players and trying to fix the play, Vindoo had gone straight to the top – to the umpire himself!

Asad Rauf Malik, aged 57, was a former first-class Pakistani cricketer and member of the Elite Panel of ICC Umpires, and appointed as an umpire for the IPL by the BCCI in 2013. As per the contract between the BCCI and Rauf, the latter was appointed umpire for sixteen matches. The contract ruled that Rauf's behaviour should be as per the Code of Conduct for Umpires. It also expected Rauf, as an umpire, to not cause any harm to the reputation of the game. The contract clearly stated, 'The umpire shall not place bets on the cricket match nor shall he persuade or induce any other person to bet on any IPL match or event'. The contract also asked of Rauf to 'not divulge the information about result of any match nor shall he accept any money, gifts or other gratification from anybody with an intention to give information in respect of weather condition, teams, condition of ground, status of match, result of match in respect of IPL season 6'.

Unfortunately, Rauf, once a fine right-handed batsman who had made headlines in Pakistan's 1986–87 domestic season for making 672 runs including a ton and five fifties, defied all of these terms.

The police stumbled upon a string of conversations between Vindoo and Rauf that made their collusion abundantly clear. From 12 April to 17 May 2013, Rauf made as many as eighty phone calls to Vindoo from his phone. Rauf's number was found registered in the name of a certain Sunil Kumar Narayanan, a Bengaluru resident who worked in a local gem shop and had provided the phone to Rauf through Sanjay Chhabra.

In the recordings of conversations that took place between 12–16 May 2013, Vindoo is heard discussing matches and betting gains and losses with Rauf and even Rauf's birthday celebration:

12 May 2013

(Match day: Rajasthan Royals vs Chennai Super Kings)

Rauf: Today is my happy birthday, please order a cake.

Vindoo: Dada, call up Sanju and tell him Dada has liked a wrist watch worth Rs 6 lakh. He keeps gifting; ask him to gift you this watch. I will call up Pawan, you call up Sanju and demand the gift.
Rauf: You say he will bring your present as well as mine and come?
Vindoo: Dada, RCB and Sunrisers should come for the finals, and if they win people will get ruined, and we will win.
Rauf: Where is the RR and CSK match (being) played?
Vindoo: In Rajasthan . . . it is still not decided, the order is yet to come. If there is an order from above, who are we? Small fry.
Rauf: He (Prem Taneja) has been saved a lot in this ongoing IPL session, who else shall let him score except us? I have told Sanjay Jaipur to take a flight and get your and my gift.[2]

In addition to the Rs 6-lakh watch, Vindoo and his team showered lavish gifts on Rauf, including a gold chain and several accessories, as is evident in this conversation:

Vindoo: Have you seen your gold chain? It's thick; if you see, you will be happy, but if you take it to Pakistan it will be a problem.
Rauf: Why?
Vindoo: Think twice, if you wear it you will be scanned at the airport. So please hide it inside the T-shirt. And ask them to give a receipt and to show they've given you a heavy discount.
Rauf: OK.

In another conversation, Rauf had asked for a bill for the gold chain, else he would have problems at Pakistan customs. It was not known whether Pawan Jaipur raised doubts on how much was being spent on Rauf, but there was a call recording during which Vindoo told Pawan they would recover the price of all the gold chains that had been gifted to Rauf if they placed bets on Mumbai.

It was clear from the recordings that Vindoo was priming Rauf for a big pay-off. This pay-off day was to be 15 May 2013, when Mumbai Indians would take on Rajasthan Royals in a match where Rauf would be one of the umpires! In the meantime, Rauf was also betting with Vindoo, making a little money on the side. Rauf was also giving lessons to Vindoo on how and how much to bet. Rauf's voice in the intercepts had been identified by two witnesses.

In a different conversation on 12 May 2013 at 9:05 p.m., Rauf was heard giving his opinion on the Jaipur pitch where the Rajasthan Royals–Chennai Super Kings match was to be played: 'This wicket is difficult.' At 10 p.m., Rauf asked Vindoo about the 'ongoing rate' and placed a bet on the match between Rajasthan Royals and Chennai Super Kings with bookie Prem Taneja. On 14 May, Rauf and Vindoo planned a lunch meeting. Rauf also spoke about betting on CSK at the rate of 40 paise in the match between Chennai Super Kings and Delhi Daredevils in Chennai. Then on 14–15 May, all of these men, including Taneja and the Chabbria brothers, sat in Room No. 409 of Hotel Oakwood in Juhu, virtually turning it into a gambling den, and began accepting bets over the phone from their contacts on the match between Rajasthan Royals and Mumbai Indians that was to be played at Wankhede on 15 May.

When the day finally dawned, Rauf called Vindoo with a message that thrilled the latter and made him feel that all his efforts were finally going to pay off. The message that Rauf was heard giving Vindoo was: '*Aaj zindagi ki haar jeet kar lo* (Today is the most important day; make the most of it).' The investigators never did find out what exactly Rauf did on the ground as an umpire during the match, but they knew without doubt he was complicit in aiding betting. This big *zindagi ki haar jeet* day turned out to be the last day for the group. The next day, panic calls flew back and forth.

On 16 May, as the first arrests took place in Mumbai and Delhi, Vindoo frantically called Rauf:

Rauf: What happened?
Vindoo: Abey, you did not watch TV news?
Rauf: What?
Vindoo: Players have been picked up. Switch off all cellphones, break the SIM cards.
Rauf: OK.
Vindoo: Three players of Rajasthan have been arrested, and there is a buzz that there are 40 more to go . . . they have got all of them . . . you take a flight and go to Pakistan, darling, I love you.

Vindoo also asked him to destroy the SIM of the phone gifted to him by Sanjay. Everyone was heard panicking about the SIM leaving a trail that would lead back to them. Pawan Jaipur was heard telling Vindoo, 'There is a problem, the SIM given to Rauf, tell him to destroy that.' He fled to Dubai with his brother on the same day, leaving their jewellery business behind. Vindoo Dara Singh was a director in their jewellery firm, Motisons Jewellers.

During a massive raid conducted in 2012 on Motisons' premises, the income tax department unearthed unaccounted money to the tune of about Rs 100 crore, plus assets and gold worth around Rs 2 crore. But at that time, the department had failed to comprehend the significance of Vindoo's connection with Motisons Jewellers, or the jewellers' connection to the international betting market.

On 20 May 2013, Asad Rauf fled to Pakistan without even getting a chance to collect his precious booty. The Mumbai Crime Branch held in its possession the bills for parcels containing branded shoes, clothes and other personal effects sent by bookie Prem Taneja to Rauf from Delhi airport's cargo section. These parcels were sent on 20 May itself. The Mumbai Police asked Air India for the custody of these bags, and they were sent to Mumbai on 23 May. The police also seized three bills, two dated 25 April 2013 worth Rs 6,000 and Rs 38,500, and one dated 26 April 2013 worth Rs 22,000, all paid for by Taneja. All the bills were in the name of Asad Malik.

Rauf may have escaped home empty-handed, but his inflated bank account, a watch worth Rs 6 lakh and gold chains aroused suspicion. From the safety of Pakistan, he issued grand statements to the effect that he would cooperate with the ICC in order to clear his name, but not with the Mumbai Police. According to him, the Mumbai Police had some 'mysterious vendetta' against him and all that he had left behind in his bags were some shells and 'sacred objects'. He went on to say that it was common for cricketers to accept gifts and it was not a crime to do so. In fact, he explained, it was the culture of the Indian subcontinent, especially among Indians and Pakistanis, to gift things to each other. 'It's a tradition in Pakistan and even in India (to give gifts). There are lots of instances when people come from India (to Pakistan), go to shops and the shopkeepers don't take the money from the guests. But I have not taken any gifts for fixing matches,' he said. Rauf denied all allegations about the controversial parcels. 'I had requested Vindoo to send those bags to the Delhi airport, but due to some miscommunication, I missed them.'[3]

As the charade continued, more sordid facts about Rauf began to emerge. Leaving India proved to be a wise decision for him, since Vindoo was arrested the very next day, and the Mumbai Police had similar plans for Rauf too. Besides, Rauf had another story going on in India that he had managed to escape.

In August 2012, Leena Kapoor, a Mumbai-based model, had filed a complaint with the Mumbai Police alleging that the much-married Rauf had sexually exploited her by promising to marry her and also giving her a shot at Hindi films.[4] The controversy had led to the release of pictures that showed both of them in hotel rooms, bedrooms and kitchens, in fairly intimate situations. Their antics were the only source of humour in an otherwise grim fixing scandal, especially when Kapoor alleged that she didn't know what Rauf was up to when visitors came in with bags full of cash.

As with the fixing scandal, Rauf outrightly denied any charges. His standard line was, 'If there is any truth in the allegations, I will come to India to face the probe.'[5] Which, of course, he hasn't till date. Rauf went on to say that the ICC and its anti-corruption wing had investigated all allegations against him and given him a clean chit. 'I have provided all my bank accounts, my property details and my SIM card details to them,' he said.

Thankfully, the ICC saw through his façade and distanced themselves from the official. The global cricketing body withdrew Rauf from officiating in the Champions Trophy in June 2013 following his involvement in the scandal, and later dropped him from the Elite Panel of ICC Umpires to which he had been appointed in April 2006. However, the governing body maintained that both instances had nothing to do with the match-fixing row and that the decision was taken after Rauf's annual review.

15

THE POWERFUL AND PROTECTED MEIYAPPAN

The spectators were restless, and not just because of the arid summer heat of Rajasthan. This was a much-awaited match, as CSK had not lost a single game batting first that season, while RR had never lost on home ground. On 12 May 2013, at 7:30 p.m., the two captains strode out to the field for the toss at Jaipur's Sawai Mansingh Stadium. RR won and chose to bowl. Would CSK continue their batting-first winning streak?

Far away from the stadium, the police sat at their listening posts. Vindoo, who by this time was already on the police radar, had led them to another name – a much bigger name that would create waves in the cricketing world: Gurunath Meiyappan, son-in-law to BCCI supremo N. Srinivasan, and 'Team Principal' of Chennai Super Kings! When the police started tracking

Meiyappan's calls, they realized he was in regular touch with a host of bookies and punters, including a Vikram Agarwal who was a hotelier and an alleged punter operating from Chennai. The police knew by now that Meiyappan would regularly place bets in IPL matches, both in favour of his team (CSK) and against.

At 7:45 p.m., the police recorded a conversation between bookie Pawan Jaipur and Vindoo, during which the former asked Vindoo to speak to Meiyappan on what he had to say about the ongoing match. The conversation wasn't sufficient for the police to bring Meiyappan in, for they needed to understand what kind of information he had been supplying to the bookies. Then, at 8:58 p.m., the call they had been waiting for came – Meiyappan called Vindoo to discuss the bets:[1]

Meiyappan: What is the current rate?

Vindoo: Rajasthan Royals at 79 paise and CSK at 81 paise. Though CSK do not look like favourites today, but they will surely win.

Meiyappan: Place Rs 20 lakh on Rajasthan Royals; I think they will win. I think CSK will put up a score of 130–140 runs only. Rajasthan Royals has a better chance.

Vindoo: Yeah, but CSK will win, you have to trust me. You just see what is going to happen. I will tell you CSK will make race runs (sic) and RR is going to lose.

Meiyappan: Can I exit, what can we do now?

Vindoo: Place bets on CSK.

Meiyappan: Are you sure CSK will win?

Vindoo: Yes.

Meiyappan: What's the rate?

Vindoo: RR at 83 paise.

Meiyappan: Okay, so place Rs 30 lakh on CSK.

The confidence that Meiyappan showed in CSK's chances was not the confidence of an ordinary cricket enthusiast. He also went on to predict how many runs CSK would make. It remained to be seen whether he would be right. At 9:10 p.m., Vindoo called bookie Pawan Jaipur:[2]

Vindoo: *Kya rate hai?* (What is the rate?)

Pawan: 80–83 (CSK at 80 paise and RR at 83 paise).

Vindoo: 30 *peti uske liye laga lo.* (Place Rs 30 lakh on behalf of Meiyappan.)

Pawan: *Maine 80 pe 30 khai* (I have accepted a Rs 30 lakh bet on the team, riding at 80 paise).

This recording showed that Vindoo and Meiyappan were constantly in touch over the course of the game. The following conversation was recorded at 9:15 p.m.:[3]

Meiyappan: How are we trading now?

Vindoo: You are losing Rs 64.20 (lakh) currently.

Meiyappan: Okay, tell me what (are) the current rates?

Vindoo: RR is at 43 paise.

Meiyappan: Okay, place Rs 30 lakhs on RR.

Vindoo then called Pawan: *Ye marega aaj; 30 lakh at 44 paise Rajasthan pe lagao.* (It looks like he will do badly. Place Rs 30 lakh on RR at 44 paise.)

In the next call, Meiyappan asked Vindoo: How are we doing now?

Vindoo: I am shivering. Forget about winning, let's now just try to balance it.

Vindoo then checked the odds with Pawan:

Vindoo: How are we trading now?

Pawan: You are losing Rs 1.23 crore on CSK and you are winning Rs 66.49 lakh on Rajasthan.

Vindoo quickly called an anxious Meiyappan:

Meiyappan: How are we trading now?

Vindoo: 1.24 crore on CSK and 55 lakh on RR.

The observant listener would figure out that Vindoo Dara Singh was making money off Meiyappan! He made a one-paisa commission on every bet he placed on behalf of Meiyappan. While quoting the odds from the bookie, he was either adding or subtracting one paisa, depending on whether Meiyappan was betting in favour of or against a team. So when the bookie told Vindoo that Meiyappan was losing 1.24 crore on CSK, it was actually 1.23 crore, and when Vindoo told Meiyappan he was winning 55 lakh on RR, it was actually 66.49 lakh.

This call would haunt Meiyappan, as the Mudgal Committee Report would refer to again and again to make a case for his guilt. What made Meiyappan lose if he was sure of CSK? The answer would come much later, when the Mudgal Committee would demand that the match be investigated further.

●

Who is Meiyappan? Known as 'Prince Gurunath' in Chennai, Meiyappan held an impeccable pedigree. His father was honorary consul for Paraguay and ex-president of Southern India Chamber of Commerce and Industry, while his mother Lalitha was an avid golfer who represented the country in the sport. If this wasn't enough, he was also the scion of the family that owned AVM Productions, one of South India's oldest film and television production houses.

Taking a cue from his mother, Meiyappan was active on the city's golfing circuit, where he met Rupa, the daughter of N. Srinivasan, who was an avid golfer herself. It has been reported that it was on the golf course he learnt the most important lessons in value and character: 'In a day's golf, you can discover much about a man's character – how he is as a person, and how he would do business. Everything.'

While his father, grandfather and father-in-law attracted public attention with regard to their involvement with AVM Productions, Meiyappan kept away from the eyes of the media to a large extent, but he wasn't an unknown entity. Within the Chennai film industry, which transcends the boundaries of commerce and reaches the realm of worship, he was a powerful figure. His marriage to Srinivasan's daughter, hailed as the merger of two of the richest families in Chennai, was the jewel in his crown.

Then on 25 May 2013, it all came tumbling down for Prince Gurunath.

That day, Mumbai Police arrested Meiyappan under the provisions of Sections 415, 420 and 417 of the Indian Penal Code, on charges of cheating and fraud. A day after his arrest, they raided his Chennai home and seized sports material (such as CSK kits), his visiting cards that described him as 'Team Principal' of CSK, and his cellphones, along with a number of SIM cards – 90031548xx, 90945546xx, 98405499xx, 72999111xx, 72999155xx – which he used to give constant updates on the day's match and also place bets.

The charges on Meiyappan were also an indirect indictment of Srinivasan and gave rise to perfectly legitimate questions on conflict of interest, since Srinivasan headed India Cement, which owned CSK. This dual position as president of BCCI and de facto owner of an IPL franchise had an immediate implication: Srinivasan would have to take disciplinary action against his own franchise and his own son-in-law.

Meiyappan, who had labelled himself 'Team Principal' on a verified Twitter account, shed this title the moment the police started tightening its noose around him. He would be present during team meetings, at the auction table, in the owner's dugout, etc. He also participated in the IPL owners' meet, travelled with the CSK team, and took part in the IPL owners' workshop projecting himself as CSK owner. He was authorized (though implicit at times) by franchise owner India Cements to participate and be present when various crucial decisions were taken in relation to CSK. India Cements itself had forwarded accreditation requests for Meiyappan every year for six IPL seasons under different nomenclatures (i.e., owner and management).

In 2011, in a representation made by CSK for accreditation to BCCI, Meiyappan was described as the franchise's director. He was in a position wherein he had easy access to sensitive team information, team strategies, details on match conditions, etc., – all in all, information that was outside the purview of an ordinary person following the game.

In his book, *Underneath the Southern Cross,* Michael Hussey, the Australian right-hander and star batsman of CSK, wrote that CSK team owner and BCCI Chairman N. Srinivasan had handed the control of the team to Meiyappan. 'Our owner was Indian Cements, headed by Mr Srinivasan,' Hussey writes. 'As he was also on the board of BCCI, he gave control of the team to his son-in-law Mr Gurunath. He ran the team along with Kepler Wessels, who was the coach.'

Hussey was quite vocal on the eve of his book launch. He said that though he did not know what exactly Meiyappan's designation was, he was very much on the field and often attended training sessions. Hussey mentioned that it was not unusual to find Meiyappan talking to Kepler Wessels, the CSK coach during IPL 2008, or to the players, at training and in hotels.

In spite of this damning evidence, something that would have been obvious to even a five-year-old that Meiyappan was indeed deeply associated with the inner workings of CSK,

Indian captain M. S. Dhoni's reaction was surprising. As the news broke that Meiyappan was one of the suspects in betting, Dhoni did the unexpected – he went along with the lie and along with BCCI Chief Srinivasan and officials of India Cements, took the stand that Meiyappan had nothing to do with cricketing affairs of CSK and was a mere cricket enthusiast supporting CSK. It was obvious to everyone, especially after the Mudgal Report would come out, that Dhoni had a role to play in the whole affair. The question was – what? Was he, in anyway, complicit, like Lalit Modi would claim?

Either way, it was clear that Meiyappan had strayed away from the values of the venerated AVM. Ironically, he was named after his legendary grandfather, A. V. Meiyappan Chettiyar, who was known for his discipline, dignity and honesty.

●

Vindoo had told the police that he had befriended Meiyappan six years previously at a cricket-related party and then stayed in touch. He had claimed it was around the same time he got addicted to betting as a sport and did not realize that he was indulging in gambling. The police had seized a laptop and an iPad that he used for betting purposes. He also handed over three phones that his bookie-friend, Sandeep Chhabra alias Pawan Jaipur, had given him before fleeing the country.

Vindoo, as it emerged from the investigation of his phone calls, played an active role in cultivating Meiyappan and passing on crucial details related to the game to the bookies.[4] In addition to the calls on 12 May 2013, several other calls were recorded between the two. On 13 May, Meiyappan informed Vindoo that the Sunrisers would win against Mumbai Indians. On 14 May, he informed Vindoo that the game between CSK and Delhi Daredevils at the M. A. Chidambaram Stadium in Chepauk, Chennai, might not take place due to the absence of the required stability certificate. On 15 May, Vindoo passed on information to Sandeep Chhabra quoting Meiyappan as saying that KKR would win against Pune Warriors. These conversations make it evident that Meiyappan not only misused his knowledge as a Team Principal of CSK, but also as someone who had a direct phone line to the BCCI top management.

But despite the damning evidence that reflected badly on the BCCI and made Srinivasan complicit, the BCCI boss repeatedly insisted he had nothing to do with Meiyappan and would not resign. He wasted no time in distancing himself and India Cements from Meiyappan, and called Meiyappan an 'honorary member of the team management' of CSK. He told the police and the public that Meiyappan was nothing more than a 'cricketing enthusiast', a claim that was roundly rejected by the Mudgal Committee Report.

It was difficult for cricket enthusiasts across the country to fathom how Srinivasan could continue to be BCCI boss when his son-in-law was at the very centre of a spot-fixing storm. As cries went up against Meiyappan and for a ban on CSK as per IPL rules, C. A. Sundaram, the senior counsel who appeared on behalf of the BCCI, stated that even if Meiyappan was acting on behalf of CSK and had resorted to betting, it was not with the approval of or with the consent of India Cements, where Meiyappan did not hold an official position. He also submitted that the team be given a punishment that was proportionate to the infraction by Meiyappan and that India Cements was not culpable. He implied that Meiyappan should face a punishment similar to the players found guilty of corruption.

As it was, the two-member probe panel appointed by the BCCI to investigate the IPL scandal, gave both the cricket body and Meiyappan a clean chit. Srinivasan, despite pressure from the media and from several former cricket officials, refused to quit as BCCI Chairman, famously declaring, 'I refuse to be railroaded. I will not resign. It's not me but my daughter who has married Mr Meiyappan. If he has done any wrong, the law will take its own course.'

But on 2 June 2013, Srinivasan did 'step aside' – resign – as BCCI Chief; however, in September 2013, he was re-elected without opposition. This was conditional to the verdict from the Supreme Court on the special leave petition filed by Bihar Cricket Association against the BCCI's probe panel instituted to probe IPL corruption. And on 28 October 2013, Srinivasan was reinstated by the Supreme Court as if nothing had ever happened. What's more, in February 2014, Srinivasan would go on to head the ICC itself!

While Hussey, in his book, did point to Meiyappan's role in CSK, he chose not to stand by his words once the book was published in September 2013. Hussey would say that he knew Meiyappan was close to CSK, but not any more than Srinivasan, who as Chairman of India Cements, owned CSK. He even stated he had no intention of questioning Srinivasan's word and that he might have been 'a little bit wrong' about Meiyappan: 'I hope to be associated with CSK in some capacity even after I stop playing. I have a fantastic rapport with everyone at CSK. I get on very well with the coach. I get on very well with the players and have had a lot of success with CSK. I thoroughly enjoyed my time there and they are a fantastic franchise. I would love to continue there in whatever capacity in the future.'[5] Wanting to leave nothing to chance, he even apologized to Srinivasan when the two happened to meet at a team dinner. And Srinivasan, a man who was known to never forgive a slight, was rather kind to Hussey, telling not to worry. 'It was all a misunderstanding,' Srinivasan reassured him.

That pretty much summed up the saga of any corrupt official in our country – it was all a misunderstanding!

16

THE SUSPECT MATCH

On 10 February 2014, the Mudgal Committee delivered its verdict on Meiyappan and stated that he was a 'team official', and pronounced him guilty of betting in his official capacity. The committee suggested that fixing charges needed 'further investigation'. They also handed a sealed envelope to the Supreme Court to be opened at its discretion, an envelope that was widely acknowledged as the 'envelope that can bring Indian cricket down', and supposedly contained the names of six players who had hitherto not been dragged into the fixing scandal – two of them fairly big names and one of whom played the World Cup that India won in 2011. The committee also recommended further investigation into the allegations of all those named in the envelope. It chose not to make the names public because it did not want to tarnish their reputations before a proper investigation.

The findings of the sealed envelope were backed by audio tapes of Tinku Mandi and Chandresh, where references to 'high-level fixing' were made and the names of two Indian players were mentioned. They claimed that these two international cricketers were in touch with Pakistan- and Dubai-based members of the betting syndicate. This information was also backed by Sreesanth during his interrogation, when he claimed that three other prominent players representing India, including left-arm seamer R. P. Singh, had been approached by bookies and were offered flats and gifts.

Surprisingly, this angle had been overlooked by the Delhi Police in its investigations, and even when the taped conversations confirmed it, they put it down to 'boasting'. Sources in the Delhi Police confirmed that R. P. Singh had indeed been summoned for questioning by the sleuths. Neeraj Kumar was the only one who stated in his deposition that further investigations should have been made regarding those references.

As the drama over the envelope and its contents dragged on, the Mumbai Police charged Meiyappan on two counts: betting in IPL matches; and passing insider information to the bookies. In support of this, taped phone conversations were cited: calls between Meiyappan and Vindoo before matches, some of them transcribed in the previous chapter, that revealed how Meiyappan revealed to Vindoo that CSK would make about 130–40 runs in a match where CSK would make 141 runs, and 'RR is winning *pucca*'; a day later, on 13 May, Meiyappan told Vindoo that the wicket at Ranchi was slower and that rain/cyclone was predicted in Chennai on that day. On 14 May, Meiyappan told Vindoo about the issue with Chepauk stadium, and that evening, told him CSK would win '100 per cent', and in another call, said, 'I am giving you the weak link in bowling.'

On the basis of these facts, the Mumbai Police accused Meiyappan of providing insider information to Vindoo in order to aid betting. The Mudgal Committee, however, refrained from levelling charges of match fixing against Meiyappan, but made a strong observation that matches involving CSK and other IPL teams were suspected to be fixed and required thorough investigation – an observation in fact made by two former presidents of the BCCI. The match played between CSK and RR on 12 May 2013 featured prominently in the Mudgal Committee Report, and the committee, in its investigation, found enough information on record to indicate that further investigation was required with regard to this match.

The report even analyzed the match ball-by-ball, and found a lot of reasons to believe that all was not right that day with CSK. To start with, the team looked relaxed as if they were not playing to win. This was later justified on the basis of the fact that they had already qualified for the finals, but an overall lack of fire was uncharacteristic of CSK, a team known for their on-field aggression.

CSK also aroused suspicion in the way it made its runs that day. After batting first and being placed at a comfortable eighty-nine for the loss of one wicket in the eleventh over, they ended up with a modest total of 141 for 4. Moreover, no sixes were hit by a team consisting of proven six-hitters. This lack of adequate acceleration, despite having an aggressive batsman like Ravinder Jadeja at the crease while CSK had six wickets to spare, was pointed out. The score also correlated with the taped conversation between Vindoo and Meiyappan, where the latter clearly predicted CSK would score between 135 and 140 runs. The fact that CSK ended up with 141 was only because the last ball was edged for a boundary.

Transcripts indicate that at the start of the match, Meiyappan thought CSK would win the match. Meiyappan, however, lost the day's bet. He had originally bet on CSK to win, but when Dhoni and Raina fell in the twelfth over, he started to cover his bets by betting on Rajasthan Royals. Transcripts would reveal that the odds by then were being continuously lowered on Rajasthan Royals, and so despite placing a huge bet of Rs 1.40 crore on Rajasthan Royals, he could not make up his loss on his wager on CSK. Ultimately, he lost Rs 60 lakh that day.

Mohammed Abdi, a sports administrator from Rajasthan and also the constituted attorney of Lalit Modi, former chairman of the IPL Governing Council, developed this issue further and placed an analysis of the match in support of his contention that it was fixed. The analysis indicated that not only did CSK, with its strong batting line-up, not score a single six while Rajasthan Royals managed nine sixes, but there was also a lack of surge by CSK towards the end of the innings, despite wickets in hand. It was alleged that the field was not properly set, keeping in mind the pace of the game, while CSK bowlers did not bowl to the field set either. It was further alleged that the batsmen threw their wickets away. It was pointed out that CSK had been consistently coming up with huge scores and there was no explanation as to why it had scored below par in the match. At the start of the 12th over, CSK was a healthy 85 for 1, scoring at a rate of around 7.7 runs per over.

Abdi, in his FIR at Jyotinagar Police Station, alleged that the match was fixed with the assistance of CSK players who were wilfully not playing to their capacity, and that they also played suicidal shots on a pitch considered good for batting.

●

If Abdi's contentions were right, the million-dollar question, of course, was whether or not the CSK team participated in the fixing. From the material that the Jaipur Police produced before the Mudgal Committee, the committee stated it was evident that no worthwhile investigation had been carried out into the match. Then there was the deposition of G. Sampath Kumar, the Superintendent of Police (Tiruchirappalli Railways, Tamil Nadu), which stated that the Q Branch CID of the Chennai Police, which looks after internal security, in the course of its investigation into a fake passport racket, had come across materials that indicated large-scale betting on IPL matches.

As per Sampath Kumar, one Utham Jain (Kitty) had been interrogated by the Q Branch in his presence on 23 May 2013, who disclosed that pursuant to a plan to fix the 12-May match between CSK and RR, he was informed by one Vikram Agarwal on 27 April at a dinner that a deal had been worked out. Kitty was also informed by Meiyappan that a senior player of CSK had agreed to play as per the plan and the team would score 140 runs. This plan was communicated to one Sanjay in Jaipur over phone by Vikram Agarwal in the presence of Kitty. The names that were part of Kitty's testimony were M. S. Dhoni and Suresh Raina.

Did this mean Dhoni was one of the six Indian players mentioned in the Mudgal Committee Report?[1] If yes, such news could have brought Indian cricket to its knees. Dhoni, after all, was the much-loved captain who gave India the World Cup in 2011. The sealed report also carried the name of Dhoni's close associate R. P. Singh, who was questioned by the Delhi Police during the investigations. If this is true, media reports and pictures of Dhoni's wife, Sakshi, sitting next to Vindoo at several IPL matches would suddenly assume a lot more significance.

A curious thing happened to the evidence, however. The Mudgal Committee was informed by the said police officer that all officers who knew the disclosures by Kitty were transferred out and the matter was referred to the Chennai Police Crime Branch. Curiously, the interrogation report of Kitty was not available in the records of the crime branch when they produced the file – Case No. 1/2013 – before the committee.

K. Bhuvaneswari, the Superintendent of Police, Q Branch CID, admitted that there was another file with the Q Branch pertaining to the investigation of a fake passport case against Mohammed Jaffar, alias Jaffarullah, in connection with the Q Branch Case No. 1/2013. The committee was assured that this particular file would be produced by the Q Branch at 4 p.m. on 1 January 2013. Surprisingly, no one appeared before the committee and no record was produced before it. The committee stated there had been absolutely no response or communication from the Q Branch thereafter, and therefore not in a position to ascertain whether the interrogation report of Kitty, as stated by Sampath Kumar, in fact existed. However, many media reports quoted Sampath Kumar confirming the existence of such a report. So the silence, in the eyes of the committee, was damning. It stated clearly that under the circumstances, in view of the curious conduct of the Q Branch and the crime branch of the Chennai Police, further investigation into this particular match was necessary.

Widening the purview of the investigations, the Enforcement Directorate (ED) registered a money-laundering case in the IPL spot-fixing scandal so as to probe the alleged routing of *hawala* funds, with other financial irregularities emerging after the police investigations. With the directorate coming into the picture by invoking the criminal clauses of the Prevention of Money Laundering Act (PMLA), the noose would tighten around accused players and bookies, as, under the Act, the onus of proving one's innocence is on the accused, along with the possibility of seizure of assets and bank accounts.

Whether or not the six players will be arraigned, the fact remains that many players, including stars, were approached by bookies during the IPL, which they failed to report to the IPL management. The fact that the BCCI failed to look into these matters will haunt them as the investigations into the *hawala* trails are bound to open up a can of worms during international tournaments in the coming years.

17

RAJ AND SHILPA

In addition to Meiyappan, the Mudgal Committee Report pointed fingers at one more person whose actions they believed needed further investigation. This person was Raj Kundra. But who was this wealthy businessman from London who nobody knew till a few years ago?

When the news of Kundra's involvement first broke in June 2013 in the aftermath of the spot-fixing arrests, all hell broke loose. Reams of newspaper print, Twitter hashtags, blogs and Facebook updates went live with the Kundra story. In two months, twenty-nine people had been accused and arrested for their alleged role in fixing matches, but few of them raised the storm that the Kundra episode did. Suddenly, the IPL seemed more tainted than ever, with its credibility questioned at fundamental levels. Why? Because Kundra, along with his celebrity-wife Shilpa Shetty, were also part owners of the Rajasthan Royals team whose players had been arrested for spot-fixing.

Kundra was an unknown entity until his marriage to Shilpa Shetty, after which he became a household name. When the couple decided to buy stake in Rajasthan Royals, the celebrity quotient of the IPL soared.

Kundra's name was brought into the controversy on the back of RR player Siddarth Trivedi's testimony. According to Trivedi, Kundra's close friend Umesh Goenka frequently came to watch cricket matches at the stadium and was seen with Kundra and Shilpa Shetty most of the time. Kundra had also introduced Goenka to RR players like Ajit Chandila. Trivedi stated that one day, Goenka called him asking for information about team composition, but he refused because he was not sure what the information was required for. He also stated that Goenka would repeatedly call him, asking for such information. And there was at least one occasion when Goenka called him and said that Kundra was aware he wanted this information from Trivedi. Kundra was said to have invited Goenka for after-match parties where he met players. Based on this statement, the police began to look into Goenka's affairs.[1]

Goenka, born in Sikkim, began his career as a trader dealing in sponge iron, and later took to stockbroking. However, he lost hugely at the bourses, so he moved to London where he became friends with Kundra. He returned to India in 2008 and started a business in the manufacture of mild steel; Kundra holds a 42 per cent share in this company, with Goenka himself holding 16 per cent.

Goenka was questioned for over four days by the Delhi Police Special Cell. He then confessed he had been betting on cricket matches over the last six years. In 2010, during the third season of the IPL, some of the matches were played in Ahmedabad, and Goenka would go to these matches in the company of Kundra. In the next season, Goenka went to watch matches in Jaipur. It was then that Kundra started discussing betting with him, inquiring about betting rates for the ongoing matches. In 2012, during IPL Season 5, Kundra informed Goenka that he intended to place huge bets on matches. Kundra then introduced Goenka to one Puneet Pahwa (Kaku) of Jaipur, who, as Kundra would have it, was a trusted bookie and could be used for placing bets.

Goenka claimed he was given instructions on betting by Kundra himself. He fixed a certain percentage of money as his cut every time Kundra placed a bet. However, the money was apparently not given to him at the time of betting, and he took his cut once Kundra paid him. Goenka also claimed that Shilpa Shetty had placed a bet on a RR game against KKR.[2] He, however, did not specify the match on which Shilpa had allegedly asked him to place a bet.

Once the name of Shilpa Shetty – the *Baazigar*-girl who had enjoyed a second shot at celebrityhood after winning *Big Brother* – was dragged into the betting controversy, the media went into a blitzkrieg. The Shilpa–Kundra angle created a furore bigger than that of Vindoo, Meiyappan or even the three cricketers themselves. Soon, Kundra was taken into custody and questioned for well over twelve hours.[3]

This was really not the news that Rajasthan Royals needed, especially after the arrest of three of its players. The scandal had overshadowed its on-field performance in that IPL season, where it finished third, their first top-four finish since their triumphant campaign in IPL's inaugural edition in 2008. Since the 2008 triumph, the Royals team had been embroiled in various controversies over the years. To begin with, the team – owned by a consortium of four business-entities – was often seen as being given special privileges by the IPL founding chairman, Lalit Modi. Suresh Chellaram, whose family owned the largest stake in the Royals, is Modi's brother-in-law. As a result, Modi's ouster from BCCI and IPL was soon followed by the BCCI expelling Rajasthan Royals and Kings XI Punjab for a breach of the franchise agreement in 2010. However, the Royals took legal recourse and were reinstated into the IPL well before the 2011 auction.

The Royals was also under the scanner for their monetary flow, with the Enforcement Directorate having issued multiple notices to them for an alleged breach of regulations. And with the three tainted cricketers coming from the RR stable, the money-ball team of the IPL was in the news more for off-field activities than for its on-field performance. Now with Kundra being questioned, the spotlight was on the entire team.

When the news of Kundra broke, Rajasthan Royals, much like CSK, played it safe. It was quick to dissociate itself from Kundra, and proclaimed in a press release: 'As a franchise, the same set of rules applied to players, management and owners. As such, our actions will be consistent as in the case of the spot-fixing allegations with respect to our players. Mr Raj Kundra is a minority (11.7 per cent) shareholder, and he has no involvement in the running of the franchise.'[4]

Kundra tweeted that the media had 'misconstrued everything';[5] he issued a statement that he had done nothing 'for which I need to have any regrets' and that he would give up his share in the franchise if proven guilty on any count – a stand he would stick to even after the Mudgal Committee Report came out. 'I have always maintained that the franchise takes a zero-tolerance approach to betting, spot-fixing or match-fixing, and I entirely and wholeheartedly endorse the same. As far as my own alleged act of commission or omission is concerned, I reiterate that I am totally innocent, and in any event I wish to make it abundantly clear that if an iota of wrongdoing is finally established against me, I would unhesitatingly forfeit my share in the franchise.'

Meanwhile, Shilpa Shetty was extremely agitated, as was evident from the stream of her tweets:

#We love cricket, it's the passion for the sport that made us a part of IPL. It's extremely disheartening to keep clarifying that.[6]

#We are wronged and have not done anything Wrong!! It's been very upsetting to see that Umesh (Goenka) has misused Raj's name. That's the true story unfortunately! We will do everything to aid the police to get to the bottom of it as a witness.

#To c news misconstrued n misreported. Pls spk 2 the Real officials in charge and get the REAL story rather than ure PAID (unreliable) sources.

#Just to reiterate, we will do all it takes to reach to the bottom of this 'spot fixing case' and be of complete help till that happens.

#For those who care, my apparent involvement in betting is complete nonsense and I have never bet on any cricket match ever. Truth will prevail.

Her final tweet on the subject was:

#Won't be saying anymore as the case is subjudice.

●

But who was this Raj Kundra who had stepped right into the maelstrom of an IPL scandal that threatened to derail the entire league?

Kundra was born into a 'simple middle-class' family in London in 1975. Kundra's father, Bal Krishan, based in Ludhiana, was asked by his father to go to London to 'earn some money and send it back to us'. Bal Krishan's first job abroad was in a cotton factory. Then he went on to work as a bus conductor. His wife worked in an optician's showroom. On days when their shifts clashed, the mother would take little Kundra and put him in the back seat of a car outside the showroom where she worked. Every three hours she would tend to him, change his nappy, refill his milk bottle, and then go back inside to work. 'My two younger sisters and I realized early that our parents were working really hard to keep us comfortable and that we needed to understand the value of money,' Kundra would say in a media interview after he became known in India following his wedding to Shilpa Shetty. 'When I was in school I would sometimes wash the family car for which dad would give me € 5,' he said. Or he would volunteer to drop something off for his father. 'That's how I learnt the value of money.'

Things turned around for the Kundras when Bal Krishan started a grocery business and later bought post offices (which is possible in Britain) and drug stores. He ventured from one business to another – if he sensed a downslide for one product, he would hop on to the next big thing.

Growing up, the biggest influence on Kundra was his father. An Indian coming to London without 'a rupee in his pocket' and without an educational background in business and yet turning himself into a successful middle-class businessman was the best fairy tale Kundra had heard as a boy. Kundra said he did not have to look beyond his home for a role model. In turn, those who now work under Kundra speak of him as a role model.

'When I turned eighten, my father gave me an ultimatum,' Kundra said. 'Either you run our restaurant or you've got six months to prove that you can do something for yourself.' The teenager then went backpacking, with a credit limit of € 2,000. His first destination was Dubai, where he met jewellery traders. Here he started new ventures, though unfortunately for him, none took off. He finally hit a jackpot when he travelled from Dubai to Nepal. That's where he discovered pashmina shawls. He bought about a hundred shawls and went knocking on the doors of Christian Dior, Joseph, and other brands, in England.

The Britons were smitten. Pashmina shawls became the rage. Kundra had a turnover of twenty million euros in the very first year, from businesses majorly included sale of shawls.[7] But soon came competition and things got tough, so Kundra returned to Dubai and got into diamond trading. He divorced his first wife, Kavita, who now lives in London with their child. One of the conditions of his divorce settlement was a privacy pact that prevents her from speaking to the media. A year after his marriage ended, he met Shilpa Shetty in London.

Kundra's family had avidly followed *Celebrity Big Brother*, a reality television show, which eventually brought Shetty international fame. Shetty's agent in the UK, who happened to be a friend of Kundra's, called him after her *Big Brother* triumph to ask his advice on her future business prospects. The agent wanted to make a movie with her in the lead, but Kundra knew that would be a mistake. Instead, he asked the agent to launch a perfume in her name. 'I told him that Shilpa is riding a wave right now, but when the film is released she might not be.'

To launch the perfume, Kundra made her an offer, but Shetty's mother informed him that her daughter had already received an offer from someone else. Kundra doubled his offer and literally bought the time that he wanted to spend with her. 'I doubled the deal, knowing that it was financially a waste . . . but it was love at first sight.'

In 2009, on their first wedding anniversary, Kundra gifted Shilpa a flat on the nineteenth floor of the world's tallest building, the Burj Khalifa in Dubai. The same year, on her birthday, Kundra bought her a two-bedroom flat worth Rs 7 crore in central London. The couple also have a seven-bedroom 'Raj Mahal' in St George's Hill, Surrey, where their neighbours include Cliff Richards and Elton John. This mansion was originally bought for Kundra's first wife, Kavita Kundra. In Mumbai, Kundra lived in Juhu in a 20,000 sq. ft-bungalow that faced the sea, and shared the address with film star Amitabh Bachchan. Suzanne Roshan, a famous interior designer and ex-wife of actor Hrithik Roshan, reportedly did the interiors, though Kundra himself owned an interior decor firm, 'Kundra and Kundra'.

He also had a taste for fast cars, and owned a Lamborghini among many others.

When the idea of an IPL team came by, people close to him advised him against buying into a team in 2009, a time of economic downturn. But he didn't pay heed. 'I'm from a country that loves football and I understand how leagues work,' he said. 'And I knew that if a football team can go from $ 1 million to $ 1 billion, then it's not long before a $ 100-million team will be worth $ 500–600 million in this cricket-crazy country.'

Kundra joined the Rajasthan Royals' board when it had a valuation of $ 100 million. Within two years, the team was said to be worth $ 200–250 million. In 2004, a UK magazine ranked Kundra the 198th-richest British-Asian. At present, he is also associated with Groupco Developers, a real-estate firm that operates in eight Indian cities; Ashwini Steel, which makes mild steel from scrap; TMT Global, which claims to predict stock prices; Essential Sports and Media, which is into production and distribution; and Iconic Investments, which claims to be a private fund trading in equity markets. There are a few other ventures too, such as Gold Gate Trading, which describes itself as a trade and investment firm based in Dubai. After coming close to bankruptcy thrice in his life, it looked like Raj Kundra really didn't want to put all his eggs in one basket.

But, in spite of all this commercial success, his reputation was taking a beating in the wake of the IPL scandal. Delhi Police Commissioner Neeraj Kumar declared to the press that Kundra had indeed placed bets through Goenka. Kundra denied these allegations, saying he had only placed friendly wagers of not more than Rs 2 lakh on some matches of IPL 6 through Goenka, after having introduced him to a bookie named Kaku. Kundra told interrogators that he had been betting for the past three years, and had so far lost around Rs 1 crore. However, he denied having approached or asking Goenka to get the players to spot-fix.

Investigators, however, did not take Kundra's claim of losing Rs 1 crore too seriously. During the questioning, sources said, Kundra claimed he had lost Rs 50 lakh in betting during IPL 4, Rs 40 lakh in IPL 5 and Rs 12.5 lakh in IPL 6. He told the police that he had placed bets on matches played only by Rajasthan Royals. However, in 2013, his team had won 11 out of the 16 matches it played, and the cops found it hard to believe his claim of losing huge amounts.

Neeraj Kumar was quick to clarify that the police had no intention of arresting Kundra merely on the basis of suspicion. 'We need material evidence to book him; merely suspecting him because his name figures in the disclosures of other arrested accused cannot be a ground to arrest him,' he said.[8] By 'material evidence', Kumar meant either direct telephonic conversation about betting or fixing the matches, or video footage that could have landed Kundra in trouble. 'In the case of the players, we had the video footage to match whatever transpired during the telephonic conversation. If that kind of evidence would have been there . . . then we would have thought of arresting him,' he said.

But while the police waited for evidence, the BCCI took action. Besides breaching the code of conduct, Kundra was also on the wrong side of the IPL's anti-corruption policy, which categorically states that any direct or indirect involvement in betting would invite suspension. Even though the word 'owner' isn't mentioned in the policy, it refers to 'Player Support Personnel': 'Any coach, trainer, manager, selector, team official, doctor, physiotherapist or any other person employed by, representing or otherwise affiliated to a playing/touring team or squad that is chosen to represent a National Cricket Federation in any Domestic Match or International Match or series of such Matches.'

On 9 June 2014, BCCI suspended Kundra from IPL, pending investigations. Kundra said in a press statement that 'he was shocked, saddened and hurt' by the decision and that he would 'fight the grounds of suspension. All those who know me are aware that sport is my first love. I own a minority 11.7 per cent share in Rajasthan Royals . . . It shocks, saddens and hurts me when my integrity towards sport is questioned, especially knowing that there are very few who have taken the initiative and been successful in the development of sport in India.' Kundra added that he trusted India's judicial system and was hopeful that he would come out clean.

Luckily for him, by the end of June 2013, the Delhi Police had made up its mind that neither Kundra nor his star wife had any direct role in the match-fixing scandal. Or, as police sources put it, there was no evidence to that effect.

The Delhi Police also decided that the match on which Kundra had allegedly placed bets took place in Jaipur, and thus he should be investigated by the Jaipur Police. Later on, the two-member BCCI probe panel of Justice T. Jayarama Chouta and Justice R. Balasubramanian, former judges of the Madras high court, absolved Kundra of all allegations and gave him a clean chit.

'We stand vindicated,' the star-couple said triumphantly. However, the triumph may have been premature. In February 2014, the Mudgal Committee expressed surprise that the Delhi Police did not take any steps whatsoever to get the statement of Kundra recorded under MCOCA, and in fact, it was only after twenty days the Delhi Police had referred the matter to the Jaipur Police for investigation. They confirmed no action was thereafter found to have been taken in connection with Raj Kundra, either by the Delhi Police or the Jaipur Police.

The Mudgal Committee suspected that there could have been an effort to cover up the involvement of Kundra in the betting scandal. In terms of BCCI regulations, even legal betting is not permitted on the part of an owner of a franchise. No benefit would accrue to Kundra by an attempt to show that bets were placed through legal betting portals based in other countries. There were materials on record, which justified an appropriate investigation to ascertain the culpability of Kundra and Shetty in placing bets as owner of a franchise in IPL. The nightmare that Kundra thought was over reappeared. However, it ended on a surprising note, with the 2015 Supreme Court Committee headed by former Chief Justice of India, R. M. Lodha, penalising Kundra with a five-year ban on any cricket activity and a suspension for life from being involved with the BCCI.

When one compared Kundra's case against that of Meiyappan's and Vindoo's, a few things stood out.

Kundra was involved in betting, whereas Meiyappan and Vindoo not only placed bets but also aided it. While Kundra's case became national news, with hundreds of tweets, blogs and analyses, Meiyappan's and Vindoo's story did not get as much play. It didn't seem to matter to the media that the duo's crime was bigger, simply because Kundra's name was bigger.

Sympathizers of Kundra and Shetty said their celebrityhood had become a liability – in the party circuit; there was always the possibility of meeting bookies or their conduits, which could easily be seen out of context. Incidentally, Kundra counted Vindoo among his good friends in Mumbai. He was present at Vindoo's house the day the latter's father, Dara Singh, passed away. Banned for life from cricket activities, former Rajasthan Royals co-owner Raj Kundra has been battling in the Supreme Court seeking lifting of the ban.

18

THE UNHOLY TRINITY

Cultural experts will tell you India is a nation obsessed with Bollywood. However, it's not just the common man. The fascination with celluloid does not dampen just because you're a celebrity yourself. There is something about Bollywood that attracts all prominent personalities, whether they are high-profile police officers, politicians, cricketers or even all-powerful gangsters. If there was a pecking order for celebrities in India, the Bollywood celebrity would win hands down.

The reason for this could be because of the massive fan following and endorsement deals that a Bollywood celebrity gets, which places them in a different league. No other career offers the opportunity to project a larger-than-life persona that grips the collective imagination.

The nexus between Bollywood and the Mumbai underworld dates back to the 1960s when Haji Mastan was a gangster to be reckoned with. For the mafia, tinsel town was not simply about charm – they had business interests in Bollywood, or the 'fillum line', as they refer to it. Back in the day, so-called 'social programmes', or public functions, hosted by underworld kingpins would see the presence of prominent stars. These programmes became great venues to discuss business and forge partnerships. In the course of working with them, Mastan soon became good friends with Dilip Kumar, Shashi Kapoor, Dharmendra, Feroz Khan, Raj Kapoor, Sanjeev Kumar, and Salim Khan.

The stars never openly talked about it but privately admitted that they had no choice but to rub shoulders with the underworld since it had so much authority that it could determine their futures and even the fate of their films. Even during the old days, there were rumours that certain stars used their proximity to the crime lords to settle scores, and to gain roles in certain films; their links with the underworld also help them project an invincible aura.

Moreover, all the infamous dons – Dawood, Chhota Rajan, Chhota Shakeel, Abu Salem, Sunil Sawant (Sautya) – had a weakness for Bollywood divas. Here too, it was Mastan who made the first foray by marrying a Bollywood starlet called Sona. According to Sona, 'Haji *saab* was extremely fond of Madhubala. Then he saw me, and my resemblance to Madhubala made him fall for me.'[1] In the course of their relationship, he also financed a few films for her and gifted her a bungalow situated near actor Dev Anand's house at Juhu. A recent Bollywood film was based on their affair.

As for Dawood, he wooed the stars to Sharjah and Dubai where they would perform in stage shows and attend private parties held at his residence. Many years later, the CBI would write a letter to the UAE government seeking details of a few Bollywood personalities who had stayed in Dubai hotels in the 1990s and reportedly enjoyed the hospitality of Dawood.

But what became even more newsworthy was Dawood's dalliance with Mandakini. The news of their affair first emerged in 1994 when the two were seen together in a photograph. Reports also claimed that she was married to him. The other newsworthy starlets in this genre have been Monica Bedi and Mamta Kulkarni. Bedi, who was studying English literature at Oxford in 1995, jumped into the Bollywood bandwagon through Manoj Kumar but success eluded her. She did a host of other films with stars like Salman Khan and Govinda, but she failed to gain ground as an actress in Bollywood. In fact, the gangster Abu Salem had tried his best to get her success.

It was a known fact that in many films financed by the underworld, the dons ordered their producers to ensure that their starlet girlfriends enjoyed a 'special status' on the sets. Sometimes, a producer would be threatened to make sure that he cast the don's girlfriend. In one such case in the late 1990s, producer Rajiv Rai was shot at and threatened by Abu Salem's gangsters. The police told the media it was a simple case of extortion. But the fact that Rai had signed up Monica Bedi for his next film had escaped the media's attention. Rai had to eventually leave Mumbai for good and settle down in Switzerland after an attempt was again made on Rai's life by Abu Salem's men in 1997.

The 1990s was not a time when Bollywood actresses posed topless in magazine covers, but Mamta Kulkarni was the pioneer. This led to the filing of a number of obscenity cases against her, and she was convicted. In 1998, she accused film-maker Rajkumar Santoshi – who directed her in *China Gate* – of molesting her. Santoshi, in turn, alleged that he had received threats from the Chhota Rajan gang – Mamta was supposed to be dating Rajan's henchman, Vicky Goswami, at the time.

As the tide turned against gangsters, ties between the underworld and Bollywood loosened. While the collusion, the grand love affairs, the business deals between gangsters and film stars seemed to have been relegated to a thing of the past, the connection of cricketers with film stars was perhaps an even older one and continued to thrive in the age of IPL.

Cricket history in India is replete with examples of happy endings as well as unfortunate divorces or separations between superstar cricketers and Bollywood glamour girls. Way before today's actresses were 'courted' by cricketers, in 1966, during an India tour, West Indies' maverick captain Gary Sobers was bowled over by Anju Mahendru, a model and upcoming actress. It was a brief affair that resulted in a secret engagement. Then there was the debonair Mansoor Ali Khan Pataudi (Tiger) married Sharmila Tagore, one of the biggest stars of the 1970s. Around the same time, Pakistan's then cricket captain Imran Khan had an affair with the 'Dum Maro Dum' girl Zeenat Aman, which didn't end as happily. The list of affairs continued: Pakistan batsman Mohsin Khan with actress Reena Roy, Vivian Richards with Neena Gupta, Sourav Ganguly with Nagma . . .

There is also no dearth of cricketers who have tried (and mostly failed) to actually become Bollywood stars themselves, starting from Salim Durani who was the first cricketer to play a lead role in a movie (B. R. Ishara's *Charitra* opposite Parveen Babi, in 1973) to Salil Ankola who made several attempts at a film and TV career, and Ajay Jadeja who did an extremely forgettable movie with Celina Jaitley in 2003. Then there was Vinod Kambli, who did a B-grade movie with Sunil Shetty (*Annarth*, 2002), then wisely decided to restrict himself to appearances as a cricket pundit in various TV shows.

The relationship between cricket and Bollywood may have changed over time, but it certainly became stronger with the launch of IPL in 2008.

●

The IPL did many things to cricket, but the biggest change was the formal infusion of Bollywood into the game. No one could deny that many KKR fans flocked to Eden Gardens to see Shah Rukh Khan and not for the cricket. The IPL, at one point, seemed to have found a formula to marry the skills of cricketers, the glamour of Bollywood and the money of India Inc. to create a carnival of entertainment. And to a large extent, that's exactly what it did. Everyone appreciated the good that Bollywood brought to cricket. Of course, the most welcoming aspect was the marketing dollars, ushering in celebrities, brand prestige, and viewers who were traditionally non-cricketing audience, like women. Cricket as a sport got more attention than it already did, and cricketers were finally stars as big as their Bollywood counterparts.

But along with the showbiz and the glamour came the IPL scandal. The endless IPL parties and social gatherings had cricketers, bookies, socialites, models and celebrities in the same room, making it a hotbed of deals. At no point in the past had cricketers been so vulnerable to the outside world. For the underworld, this was the perfect recipe for business. It was said that after the underworld got active in betting and match-fixing, bookies were given a specific brief from their bosses: Get closer to film stars or starlets, and use them to gain proximity to the players.

The honey-trap may have been implemented in the past too, but it was noticed for the first time after the arrest of bookie Ramesh Vyas and the questioning of Kundra. Vyas told the investigators that he, along with several other bookies like the Jaipur brothers who fled the country, were present at several IPL parties, including those at Hotel Oakwood and Sun-n-Sand in Mumbai. Investigators have said that it was precisely this select circle of celebrities – cricketers, their 'mutual friends' and Bollywood stars or starlets – that bookies or underworld elements would look upon as their 'access cards' to players who could be induced to fix matches. The bookies, police sources said, used this connection to flaunt or bluff targeted players to fix games, as one may or may not have known what the other person was up to.

Police sources also said that Kundra admitted to them there were many people – and some of them could have been bookies – who attended IPL parties along with the invited guests. 'We had no control over them because they would come in along with the people we had invited.' It was at one such party that Sakshi Dhoni had introduced Bollywood actress Neetu Chandra to 'mutual friends' in the cricket circle. Chandra had been linked to 21-year-old Pakistani bowler Mohammad Asif, who was banned after the 2010 spot-fixing scandal. Asif was eventually convicted through the confessions of his ex-girlfriend Veena Malik, herself a Bollywood starlet. Perhaps miffed at being dumped, she had spilled the beans, saying that Asif had been 'fixed' by cricket photographer Dheeraj Dixit, who retaliated by saying that it was Veena who was the 'glamour go-between' for fixer Mazhar Majeed, who wanted to recruit new players and had approached Dixit to get close to the cricketers. All of these introductions, fixings and relationships were seeded at the IPL parties.

Malik, investigators said, was precisely the sort of celebrity underworld elements looked upon as their 'access cards' to players who could be manipulated to fix matches. It seemed as though the parties for cricketers thrown by the don Sharad Shetty and the parties of Haji Mastan for Bollywood had fused together in a whole new avatar. All the underworld now had to do was to let loose their conduits who would mingle freely in these parties. These conduits were not small-time bookies, but rich businessmen and designated socialites, people like Vindoo and Malik, who were semi-famous and therefore beyond reproach. It was easy for these conduits to leverage known Bollywood actors as knowing or unknowing catalysts, and earn the friendly attention of young sports stars. To make things easier, women, drugs and alcohol were freely available, and in this environment of fast money, big names and bigger pay cheques, how difficult could it be to connect the dots? It's easy to see how players, who are essentially young, impressionable boys from small towns hankering for success and money, could get swayed by these big celebrities. It would not be wrong to argue that the IPL culture, its format, its alliance with showbiz, the underworld's increased access to players, all combined make the league a hotbed for betting and match-fixing.

Contrary to the old configuration where cinema had exclusive relationships with criminals and cricketers, all of them seem to have fused under the colourful and glittering IPL umbrella. At the forefront are cricketers and movie stars hobnobbing with each other, creating a symbiotic bond, and in the shadowy background, represented by bookies, are the criminals who are orchestrating the economics of the betting, deciding the odds and getting more than their fair share of the IPL money-making machine!

It would be simplistic and reductive to say that the IPL is solely to blame. Match-fixing in cricket existed before the IPL. But no one can ignore the fact that the whole set up has become more pliable because of it. As it stands now, after the IPL scandal, it wouldn't be a stretch to say this unholy triumvirate of cricketers, celebrities and criminals, has sullied a sizeable aspect of the game by planting seeds of suspicion about what could actually happen within the twenty-two yards. But what was more surprising, even after all these revelations, was the attitude of the governing body for cricket in India, under a defiant chairman, to the scandal that had erupted all around IPL and the cricket. And for that, one must understand how the BCCI could afford to get away with its reactions after the scandal was unearthed.

19

WHAT IS THE BCCI?

In 1912, an all-India cricket team visited England for the first time, sponsored and captained by the Maharaja of Patiala, and featuring the best cricketers of the time from India. Then in 1926, two representatives of the Calcutta Cricket Club travelled to London to attend few meetings of the Imperial Cricket Conference, the predecessor to the current International Cricket Council. Although technically not official representatives of Indian cricket, they were allowed to attend by Lord Harris, Chairman of the conference. The outcome of the meeting was the MCC's decision to send a team to India, led by Arthur Gilligan, who had captained England in the Ashes.

Subsequently, in a meeting with the Maharaja of Patiala and others, Gilligan praised Indian cricket and promised to press for its inclusion in the ICC if the promoters of the game in India came together to establish a single controlling body. An assurance was given, and a meeting held in Delhi on 21 November 1927, which was attended by delegates from Sindh, Punjab, Patiala, Delhi, United Provinces, Rajputana, Alwar, Bhopal, Gwalior, Baroda, Kathiawar and Central India. A consensus was reached to create a board of control for cricket in India. Another meeting, on 10 December 1927, reached a unanimous decision to form a 'provisional' board of control to represent cricket in India. Finally, in December 1928, some sports enthusiasts in Tamil Nadu came together and formalized a body called the Board of Control for Cricket in India despite only six associations affiliated to it, while the earlier decision had been to have eight. R.E. Grant Govan was made its first president and Anthony De Mello its first secretary. In 1940, it was registered under the Societies Registration Act, 1860, and later, it was registered under the Tamil Nadu Societies Registration Act, 1975, and came into effect on 22 April 1978.

Today, the BCCI has 27 state association members and three non-playing members across five zones, namely the North, South, East, West and Central Zone in India. With the help of these, it organizes several cricket tournaments in the country, like the BCCI Corporate Trophy, the Irani Cup, the N. K. P. Salve Challenger Trophy, the Ranji Trophy, the Duleep Trophy, the Vijay Hazare Trophy, the Deodhar Trophy, and the controversial Indian Premier League, which in recent years has shone the spotlight on the cricketing body more than at any other time.

In fact, if we consider the overwhelming public opinion in recent years about the BCCI, we cannot avoid the word 'authoritarian'. But cricket lovers should be thankful to Srinivasan, for it was during his high-handed and almost despotic regime that the BCCI turned into the single-most important entity in the whole IPL fixing-scandal.

The main sponsor of BCCI, Sahara Chief Subrata Roy, has also been its biggest detractor. He was the first to accuse the BCCI leadership of big egos and high-handedness. At the time, the BCCI had terminated Pune Warriors' contract over non-payment of a bank guarantee amounting to Rs 170 crore. Roy alleged that the BCCI had tricked them, leading to the termination of their IPL team. 'For three years, the board kept telling us to play, and wait for arbitration while they simply did not allow the arbitration process to start.' He placed the blame squarely on BCCI's 'arbitrary' reduction in the total number of IPL matches from that which was stipulated originally. 'They had said 94 matches will be held every season but then arbitrarily reduced the number to 74. We had made the bid for the IPL franchise based on the representations of BCCI which were false,' Roy said.[1]

In other words, Roy was echoing the opinion of several others who found the BCCI to be a body that could not be challenged, and one that worked beyond the realm of reason. No matter what storm, what accusations or corruption scandals arise, they all simply disappear into thin air the moment they reach the boardrooms of the BCCI, even if the accused in police custody happened to be the son-in-law of the BCCI president himself!

'If the chief of any institution can create and allow bad examples like Gurunath, how can a body function independently? Had Gurunath been an owner or principal of some other team, what would have happened to that team?' Roy asked. He went on to say that, 'After this example, BCCI has lost the right to take action against anyone. Their whims and fancies are more important to them than anything else. God bless BCCI!'

Subrata Roy did not restrict himself to mere words. He took action. The Sahara Group stopped sponsoring the Indian team after its contract term expired on 31 December 2013. Sahara had paid around Rs 3.34 crore for every Test, ODI and T20 match that India had featured in for the past decade. Roy went on record saying that the BCCI would suffer a colossal financial loss once Sahara pulled out. What's more, he stated that no corporate entity would be interested in spending such exorbitant amounts on cricket at a time when there seemed to be no method to the madness.

After the Meiyappan episode, the spotlight had shifted on the very administration of cricket itself. So far, only the players and bookies had been the targets, and all investigations had ended in a few arrests and a ban on the suspected players. But Meiyappan's involvement meant the corporate sponsors and the administrators were under the scanner now. They faced the heat more than the others as there were larger stakes. Politicians found this trend 'disturbing'; some of them 'advised' Srinivasan to step down. But no significant politician from any mainstream political party – be it the Congress or the BJP – vehemently and openly criticized Srinivasan's actions and asked him to quit. Even the Parliament – which had debated the 2000 match-fixing scandal, and where, ironically, sat one of the main accused of that scandal, Mohammad Azharuddin, who was banned for life by the BCCI for fixing matches – did not have much to say about Srinivasan or the board.

In the public domain, anger was evident; newspapers, television studios and social networking sites abounded with criticism. A

Mumbai citizen petitioned a local court; a cricket body raised it in the Supreme Court. Almost everybody, other than Srinivasan's associates, wanted Srinivasan to go.

But nothing happened. Srinivasan was unfazed, declaring, 'There is no law, no rule that requires me to step down. I have done no wrong. I refuse to be bulldozed. I am not going anywhere. The law will take its own course.'

But what law?

Though the Supreme Court judges wondered how Srinivasan could continue to be BCCI president, they could not go beyond asking him 'not to be in the chair'. The BCCI was free to make its own arrangement. The board cleverly got former chief Jagmohan Dalmiya 'to be in the chair' notionally, while Srinivasan remained the signing authority for everything, including cheques. After a very brief period, even that pretence was dropped and Srinivasan returned after he was re-elected.

How did this happen? Is the BCCI above the Parliament? Or the Union Ministry of Sports? Or the Supreme Court of India?

In the worldview of a layman, the Parliament is supreme. He knows that the Parliament makes laws. He knows that even if the Supreme Court ordered the Government of India on any issue, the Parliament could enact a law, pass a legislation and overrule the court's order. He knows there are constitutional bodies like the Election Commission of India, which, thanks to the bulldog approach of an earlier Chief Election Commissioner, T.N. Seshan, makes him believe that they will act against MPs and MLAs if they were in the wrong. And even the EC is not above the Supreme Court or the Parliament.

Then why is the BCCI above the law? What kind of a special body is the BCCI that it is allowed to work as if it is a law unto itself? What really is the BCCI?

●

As mentioned above, the BCCI was registered as a society, and its constitution provides for annual elections at its Annual General Meeting (AGM) for all posts, with a bar on re-election of an incumbent president beyond two consecutive years, 'provided that the General Body may in its discretion re-elect the same person as president for the third consecutive year'. To become a member of a state-level association, like for example, the Mumbai or Delhi Cricket Association, one needs to be introduced by another member and also pay an annual fee. The state-level clubs select their representatives (secretaries) who, in turn, select the BCCI officials.

The BCCI is as much a bundle of contradictions as it is an enigma. In 2005, the BCCI came up with a vision document titled 'The Cricket Board in the 21st Century'. The paper asked itself 'if, the BCCI, as the richest body in world cricket, has fulfilled its obligations towards the players and the paying public.' And it gave the expected answer in an entirely dramatic way: 'For that, we all need to introspect and touch our hearts before saying "yes, we have"!'

The vision document further said: 'For the BCCI, the buzzword should be transparency. There can't be a better start to the new-look board than resolve, that everything we do from here on, will be transparent and in the game's as well as public interest; be it election, or allotting television rights or the team selection.'

Ironically, the BCCI continues to be shrouded in mystery till date, despite its actions being subject to scrutiny and suspicion. It remains a close-knit body, with its activities known only to a select group of members or those closely connected to them. There is no way for anybody, even on the ringside, to know how a particular company bagged the home television rights or the IPL telecast rights, or why a particular player was dropped despite being in great form, or why a popular player was allowed to play in the hope of achieving records despite consistent failure, match after match. The appointments of professionals like coaches, physiotherapists and selectors are made more or less in an arbitrary manner. Their names are suggested by the BCCI members and its affiliate units whose knowledge and insight into cricket may be questionable.

BCCI throws up more questions and mysteries than it or anybody can answer. The title itself, Board of Control for Cricket in India, sounds like it could be a government undertaking under the Union Sports Ministry, or at least some kind of public authority. The Department of Sports under the Union Ministry of Youth Affairs and Sports gives recognition to sports federations every year. The department recognized forty-three such federations in 2011, but cricket was not among them.

What this means is to the layman, it seems that the BCCI is a government body, but it isn't one. It's in fact not answerable to the government at all.

Why would the BCCI not want to get recognized under the Union ministry? Surely, being a government body has its benefits.

But the reason for this is that in the current framework, the BCCI can work without being monitored or held accountable. Whenever they are dragged to court, and the court questions its arbitrary ways, they are quick to declare: 'We are a private body not affiliated to any government or its arms.'

For example, in the 2005 case involving Zee Telefilms Ltd versus the Union of India, the Centre had told the Supreme Court's five-judge bench that it had granted de facto recognition to the BCCI as the apex national body for regulating the game of cricket in India. However, the BCCI simply denied that the government had granted any recognition to it! Finally, the judges held that the BCCI was not an instrument of the state, even though it exercized public duties or state functions: 'It is a private organization whose objectives are to promote the game of cricket. Its functions are regulated and governed by its own rules and regulations independent of any statute and are only related to its members.' The five-judge constitution bench, by a 3:2 ruling, ruled that it would not be correct to classify BCCI as 'state' and make it amenable to the jurisdiction of the constitutional courts, though it allowed a small window for persons aggrieved by the BCCI's actions to move the higher courts.

Earlier, in another case, the Supreme Court had held that due to the enormity of power exercised by the BCCI, the board needed to follow the doctrine of fairness and good faith in all its activities, and that was its duty to act reasonably. But this was only an opinion (even if it is the opinion of the highest court of the country) and it was to be practised in 'good faith' – a phrase that has absolutely no meaning in a court of law.

This seems all the more absurd when one realizes the BCCI is in control of enormous amounts of public funds without any concomitant rules, regulations or laws that govern the method in which public funds are to be utilized. A BCCI office bearer, unlike public servants who deal with public funds, is not held accountable for his activities. And yet, how does one explain the fact that it often uses government-owned stadia across the country at a nominal annual rent?

The nominal rents are just one of the government benefits BCCI avails of. On 14 December 2011, in a written statement submitted to the Central Information Commission (CIC), the Union Ministry of Youth Affairs and Sports maintained that the BCCI was at par with other national sports federations and had been availing itself of various government benefits, such as customs duty and income tax exemptions. Describing this as indirect funding of the BCCI, the government asked the CIC to treat the board as an entity financed substantially by the government, and therefore, qualifying as a 'public authority' under the RTI Act. It pointed out that all civic and security services were provided by the Central or State governments concerned for organizing BCCI events. The hidden costs on security, visa clearances and so on were borne by the centre and the state governments concerned, the ministry told the CIC. Many state governments have provided land to the BCCI at concessional rates – much below the prevailing market prices – for the construction of cricket stadia. The ministry claimed that the BCCI was performing functions akin to state functions and also performing public duties by selecting national teams and representing India in international events.

The BCCI has even managed to avoid taxes on its income, claiming exemption as a charitable organization. Although the Income Tax Department withdrew this exemption in 2007–08, the BCCI only paid tax amounting to Rs 41.91 crore ($ 6.7 million) against its tax liability of Rs 413 crore ($ 66 million) in the 2009–10 financial year. This is despite the fact that global media rights for international cricket to be held in India between March 2010 and March 2014 were awarded to the production house Nimbus for $ 612 million. The official kit sponsorship rights for five years (2010–13) were awarded to Nike for $ 43 million. Air Sahara became the official Indian team sponsor for a period of four years at a cost of $ 70 million. The media rights for 25 neutral-venue ODIs to be played over five years were awarded to Zee Telefilms for $ 219.15 million. Besides, there was revenue generation to the tune of thousands of crores by way of sale of other rights, including hotel, travel and ground sponsorship. And yet the BCCI applied for exemptions on grounds beyond the understanding of a reasonable person.

The result is that despite government patronage in a country where a billion people treat cricket as a religion, nobody can question the BCCI about the rules it makes for cricket, the players it selects – some despite their consistently bad performances – the format of the game, the choosing of venue and, most importantly, how it uses the money it collects by way of these matches.

So then, to answer the question what exactly is the BCCI, the answer is seemingly simple, yet complex: the BCCI is nothing more than a society, registered by some 'sports enthusiasts'.

This answer hides more than it reveals, and it stands as a paradox. But that's exactly what the BCCI is. Even if it is merely a registered society of some businessmen, its legal status continues to be an issue of a raging debate.

●

Similarly, the relationship between the International Cricket Council (ICC) and BCCI is rather peculiar. As its member, BCCI would be expected, or rather hoped, that it would have to operate within a clear set of rules. After all, it is as a member of this body that the BCCI derives its authority to select players, umpires and officials to participate in international events and exercise control over them. It is as a member of this body that the BCCI's consent is required in hosting competitive cricket involving BCCI-contracted players within or outside the country.

But it may come as a surprise that the BCCI manages to call the shots even within the ICC. As India is by far the biggest market in terms of international cricket revenue, the BCCI's opinions tend to hold sway within the ICC's decision-making process, with other cricketing nations unwilling to oppose due to the potential loss of financial benefits. As a result, the BCCI can, and has, even taken on the ICC when it wishes. These include scheduling, player suspensions and ICC appointments. After the controversial 2007–08 Sydney Test between Australia and India, the BCCI suggested the withdrawal of the controversial umpire Steve Bucknor for the rest of the tour, and suggested replacing him with New Zealand umpire Billy Bowden. Additionally, the immediate three-match ban imposed on Harbhajan Singh for alleged racial abuse was suspended and later lifted after the charges were proven to be false in an ICC disciplinary hearing. In fact, the hearing was initiated only after the BCCI threatened to withdraw the Indian team from the tour unless the ban was lifted. The BCCI was at the time accused by other cricketing nations of unfairly utilizing its power to pressure the ICC into making concessions for it, whilst the ICC in turn was accused of being 'spineless'.

In recent times, the BCCI has been at odds with the ICC on the Future Tours Programme. It has entered into unilateral arrangements to allow more series between India, Australia and England. Funds are believed to be a major cause of dissent – the BCCI wants a lion's share from ICC's earnings since a major chunk of it is generated by way of matches organized by the BCCI. But the role of ICC as a governing body for the BCCI is no longer even a valid argument. The very man who compromised the BCCI and whose resignation had been demanded time and again controlled the ICC as chairman till September 2015. Srinivasan, in fact, was revamping the ICC to prepare for BCCI's ascendance in the world body. The man, who had faced a slew of charges, including serious ones of mismanagement, corruption and undue favours, ruled the apex body of cricket for an entire year and a half.

20

HOW THE BCCI CONTINUES TO GROW

In February 2014 in Singapore, then BCCI President N. Srinivasan mustered the support of eight full ICC members to become the Chairman. The cricket boards of Pakistan and Sri Lanka abstained from voting, and South Africa, which had initially objected to the revamp proposals, calling them 'fundamentally flawed', finally toed India's line. Sri Lanka, which was at the forefront of opposing Srinivasan's elevation, would pay the price for its stance. Only one current Sri Lankan cricketer was bought at the IPL 2014 auction. In the capped players' list released by the IPL for the seventh edition auction, there were no Pakistani cricketers, and South Africa got its reward for withdrawing the protest. It was declared as an alternative venue.

This was a small instance of the power that Srinivasan and, de facto, the President of BCCI yielded. The obvious question was: where did the power of BCCI come from? It came from two things alone: money and politics.

The BCCI earned a profit of $ 49.996 million in 2011–12, leaving the second-placed England and Wales Cricket Board (ECB) far behind. The ECB earned a net profit of just $ 24.306 million during the same period. The difference: $ 25.689 million.

However, ECB was the biggest revenue earner with $ 230.336 million amongst the ten Test-playing countries, even more than the BCCI, which earned $ 140.079 million in the same period. But ECB's expenditure ($ 206.029 million) was much more than BCCI's ($ 90.082 million), pushing it to second position on the table.

In fact, BCCI had absolutely no competition when it came to the 'all-time' net worth. As of 31 March 2012, it had a net worth of $ 294.219 million. Interestingly, BCCI's net liabilities ($ 343.834 million) were also the highest amongst the ten full members. The second-richest board was South Africa Cricket (CSA), whose net worth was $ 68.436 million on 31 December 2012. In other words, BCCI's net worth was a whopping $ 225.783 million more than CSA's. The ECB was third with $ 58.013 million.

Surprisingly, South Africa, the world No. 1 in Test cricket, was the only other country, apart from Zimbabwe, that ended in the red that year. The CSA showed a loss of $ 6.027 million, despite earning revenues worth $ 60.508 million. Also, CSA, along with Zimbabwe, was the only national board whose expenditure ($ 66.536 million) was more than the revenues it earned.

No other country comes close to India if we take a look at the accounts of some of the prominent teams in the cricket world.

Cricket Australia was the second highest revenue earner with $ 177.982 million, but since its expenditure was also huge ($ 173.163 million); its profit was limited to US$ 4.818 million. This meant only the BCCI, Australia and the ECB earned revenues over $ 140 million. The poorest national board, not surprisingly, was Zimbabwe Cricket (ZC), which showed a net worth of a mere $ 31,655. During the period in question, Zimbabwe earned $ 20.482 million in revenues, while its expenditure was $ 22.784 million, handing it a loss of $ 2.301 million.

If one left Zimbabwe out, New Zealand Cricket (NZC) was in the worst financial condition. NZC was at the bottom of the list of net profit earners at a mere $ 2.285 million, and its net worth stood at $ 8.611 million, also the lowest among the nine national boards, excluding ZC.

Such figures show the BCCI's economic power is enormous as a regulator, and enable it to pick winners. In financial terms, it has gained tremendously from the IPL format. There is virtually no other competitor in the market, nor is anyone allowed to emerge due to the BCCI's strategy of monopolizing the entire market. For every match it organizes, it collects money from the public, advertisers and sponsors. It has a monopoly over the game of cricket in India.

But all said and done, it still owes its riches to the participation of the public in its events.

So should it continue to function like a private body? Should it not be brought under the ambit of the Right to Information Act? Should the general public not know about its functioning? Should it not at least publish its audited accounts on its website?

It was precisely for these reasons that Kirti Azad, a former player, alleged that the BCCI's power came from the politicians who are part of it or those who pulled the strings from behind the curtains. When the BCCI probe panel absolved Meiyappan and Raj Kundra of any wrongdoing, Azad slammed the board and the IPL management. 'I don't blame Jagmohan Dalmiya or Srinivasan for this. The politicians are hell-bent on making BCCI the next Indian Olympic Association. We have seen what happened to IOA due to political interference and now the same is happening with BCCI. While the Mumbai Police and the Delhi Police are investigating the case, the BCCI panel has given them a clean chit. Is BCCI above the law and constitution of the country?' he asked.[1]

Experts point out it is not without reason that politicians across parties want to head state cricket bodies and then go on to become the President of the BCCI. Azad felt the BCCI should be immediately brought under the ambit of the Right to Information Act. 'There is no other alternative. The government has to intervene and bring BCCI under the RTI. When former sports minister Ajay Maken brought the Sports Bill, the Cabinet ministers involved with BCCI opposed that. If BCCI claims that they do auditing of their accounts, then why do they hesitate to come under RTI?' Azad asked. 'It is time to make BCCI function more transparently, and it can be done through RTI.' He also said that it was wrong to penalize the players while giving clean chits to the officials. 'Whenever something happens, players get penalized and officials walk free. It's a pity because despite all the controversies, cricket is still the most popular game in the country due to the hard work and excellent performance of players.'

Cricket in India has always been patronized by politicians and there could ostensibly be nothing wrong about it. In fact, they could help the game by promoting it. However, in this case, it seems to be the other way round: it looks like, at least in India, cricket is a self-sustaining billion-dollar industry that awards power to politicians than seek it from them. And among all the politicians who have headed the BCCI, Nationalist Congress Party supremo Sharad Pawar has faced the most heat. In fact, he was the one who turned around the fortunes of the BCCI by roping in Lalit Modi to come up with a concept like the IPL. Pawar could not obviously be faulted for bettering the fortunes of the BCCI.

But the kind of money that came along with the IPL also brought along other elements who had so far looked at cricket as a mere pastime and a way to make a quick buck. In the dark world of crime, till the appearance of the IPL, match-fixing and betting were not looked upon as stand-alone options that gave good returns. The investment was hardly anything.

Only once the IPL took shape did cricket become purely a money game, beginning with the auction of players. When Lalit Modi took over as the Vice President BCCI in December 2005, under the leadership of Sharad Pawar, he turned the wheel around, declaring, 'The IPL would soon become the single largest revenue-earning avenue for BCCI.'

His words would prove to be prophetic. But ironically, Modi himself did not foresee his abrupt exit. The irony was further amplified when he became the biggest detractor of the BCCI. When he recently tried to make a re-entry into Indian cricket from

Rajasthan, the BCCI left no stone unturned to prevent it. Modi had to leave the country and settle in London 'fearing for his life' from 'anti-national elements', and is waiting for a chance to come back. In fact, in the light of the Mudgal Committee revelations, Modi was the torchbearer for asking the BCCI uncomfortable questions on its laws and 'coterie' attitude, forgetting that it was he who had framed these laws and encouraged this very attitude.

Only recently has this duality of the BCCI as a private body availing government benefits begun to be questioned. The Lucknow-bench of the Allahabad High Court wondered, hearing a case in 2012, how it could do so and issued a notice to BCCI demanding a response for availing of central government's privileges and benefits while refusing to be recognized as a government body in the form of a national sports federation. The court had also asked the Centre to furnish the previous five-years' details of grants and benefits disbursed for the development of cricket, the national game hockey and other prominent sports of the country. It also asked the Union Sports Secretary to file an affidavit in this regard. A division bench comprising Justice Uma Nath Singh and Justice V. K. Dixit had passed the above order on a public interest litigation filed by an IPS officer Amitabh, and his wife, Nutan.

Their petition demanded, 'The Central government should be directed to ask the BCCI to get recognized as a national sports federation, and in case it declines to do so, the government should strip it of all the privileges and benefits. The Centre should further ask any other cricket association of the country to obtain recognition as NSF.'

Their PIL raised important questions:

1) The BCCI says it is a private body and refuses to come under the purview of the Right to Information Act, but also declines to be answerable either to the public or to the government. How can it frame rules for the regulation of cricket in the country without any authority?
2) As a private body with no government nominated head, the BCCI cannot nominate its players for national awards like the Arjuna Award, because, according to Central government directives, only sports federations recognized by the government can send in nominations. But the reality is the opposite, as cricketers head the list of Arjuna Award winners and other government recognitions.
3) The BCCI should be prevented from using the word 'India' in its name as it gives an impression that it is a government body, when, in fact, it is not. How can the BCCI call its team Team India when the government had no say in the selection of any player?

During the hearing of this PIL, the government submitted that while it wanted the BCCI to get recognition as a sports federation, 'it was not applying for the same'. Among other things, this meant that the government declared itself helpless. To give a simple analogy: the Indian government has the legislative power to take over the land of a farmer if he refuses to surrender it for a proposed government scheme like an airport or a dam. But the same government does not have enough power to bell a cash-fat cat called the BCCI.

But things may be changing. The government for some time now has been highlighting the need for bringing about reforms in the management and governance of sports to make them more responsive, responsible and result-oriented. A draft bill was proposed to the Cabinet in 2011. The Cabinet revised the bill and sent it to the national sports federations, seeking their comments and suggestions, besides calling upon the public to do so.

After this drill, it was again thought that the bill still needed some more revisions. Under the aegis of the sports ministry, a working group was constituted, headed by Justice (retd) Mukul Mudgal to prepare a revised draft of the National Sports Development Bill. The working group included eminent sportspersons like Abhinav Bindra and Viren Rasquinha, as well as sports administrators and legal experts. They held several meetings and deliberated upon the various aspects associated with the matter, and handed over the revised draft to the sports ministry in July 2013.

Among other things, the proposed National Sports Development Bill, 2013, talked about streamlining the functioning of sports bodies, delineating responsibility for bidding for international multi-sport events, devising in-house mechanism to address grievances, advising the conduct of national games at regular intervals, and suggesting that sports bodies should function as a public authority under the RTI, and mandatorily submitting reports to the Parliament. It also proposed to constitute an Appellate Sports Tribunal, with the selection committee consisting of the Chief Justice of India or his/her nominee judge, as well as the Secretary of Department of Sports. An Ethics Commission to enforce a Code of Ethics and a Sports Election Commission to conduct free and fair elections was also a must, the bill said.

However, one must note that all these changes were regarding the National Olympics Association and regarding sports that came under its aegis – it did not mention the BCCI or cricket by name. In the section where it proposed a two-fold system for functioning of national sport federations, one hoped that the BCCI would be included, but it was made clear that the BCCI is not an NSF.

The Bill stated that all federations seeking direct or indirect funding would need to be accredited by the government and would have to comply with the accreditation requirements. Since the BCCI did not seek funds, and only sought income tax rebates at times, this too did not apply to it.

The bill also said the right to represent India was reserved for Indian citizens. But the IPL has players from over eight countries as of now, and the BCCI had never claimed any of the teams represented India.

The bill also said that in order to represent India at international events and to have the right for a particular federation to use 'India' or 'Indian' in their discipline, the federation would have to comply with Chapter IV (Unethical Practices in Sports) and Chapter IX (Applicability of Right to Information Act). This was the only means through which the BCCI could possibly be dragged into court. If roped in, the BCCI would be given parameters and guidelines that applied to other NSFs. These were international practices that were time-tested; they could not be said to be draconian and intrusive to the autonomy of the so-called private bodies.

●

It should be apparent by now, even to the most idealistic sports enthusiast, that it's well-nigh impossible to nail the BCCI.

The CBI investigation ordered by the Central government in 2000 in the wake of the Azhar match-fixing scandal was to examine the role and functions of the BCCI to evaluate whether it could have prevented the alleged malpractices. Very significantly, the CBI investigation concluded that the BCCI was the single largest beneficiary of the enormous commercial success of the sport in this country, and thus, it would be the elementary duty of anybody purporting to be the apex regulatory body of a sport to keep a close watch on the performance of the team, and to thoroughly investigate into the slightest rumour, leave alone suspicion, of any malpractice.

The BCCI, however, did not care to even investigate the allegations, which were well within their ambit. For example, there was a serious controversy over a slowdown in run rate in an India vs West Indies ODI in 1994. Nayan Mongia and Manoj Prabhakar scored 11 runs in 48 balls, chasing the West Indies' total. Both players were dropped for the next match on charges of indiscipline. This match was investigated by the Justice Y. V. Chandrachud Commission following allegations of fixing.

In the recent case of Meiyappan and the controversial CSK–RR match, when the BCCI sought to investigate allegations of match-fixing, it put together a slapdash panel which gave a clean chit to all parties without due diligence. It was only the Mudgal Committee that called the BCCI bluff and found Meiyappan 'betting in an official capacity'. It described him as a CSK official in no unclear terms, thus rubbishing the earlier defence of him being 'just a cricketing enthusiast'. It also concluded Meiyappan also passed on insider information.

Justice Mukul Mudgal, however, stated that the committee didn't have enough to prove that Meiyappan had fixed matches. It ended its verdict with this suggestion: 'The allegations of fixing require further investigations.' So, the case has not yet been put to rest, and Meiyappan may yet be found guilty on other counts. However, Srinivasan's continued reign was baffling. Imagine a minister whose son in-law was arrested for taking bribes; or a CEO whose son-in-law got caught for insider trading. It is inconceivable that the minister or the CEO would not have been fired.

But the BCCI maintained a resolute indifference to the scandals erupting around the game. That made the apex body of Indian cricket a suspect; it defied credulity to believe that the BCCI was oblivious to the rampant corruption in the sport.

But over the years, not just cricket but a whole lot of other sports have been cursed with the spectre of arrogant, unethical, self-serving bosses. So can there be any remedy in the case of the BCCI? Three possible solutions are being bandied about: nationalize the body; professionalize its management; or let former cricketers run it.

Nationalization wouldn't work. The last thing cricket needs is the bureaucracy running the sport, with their political masters encircling it like vultures. Professionalizing the board seemed an interesting proposition, but isn't viable either. What could a professional CEO or a few MBAs do in an organization dominated by politicians and businessmen? The IPL has a CEO, but that has no way made it clean.

Ex-cricketers running the BCCI? It's a heart-warming thought, but is there any evidence to suggest former players make efficient administrators? Won't the sponsors, broadcasters, the ICC and other boards run rings around them? Having the heart in the right place isn't enough; you need a good head.

A real solution calls for a radical restructuring of the character, the ownership and management of the board. Convert the BCCI into a 'for-profit' public-limited company and list it on the stock exchanges with a consortium owned by the government, private bodies, sporting bodies and common fans of cricket.

It is indeed a business of sports, so let us run it like one. Strong laws would govern it. And with that, worries of betting and fixing would subside.

As the BCCI is a money-making machine that can generate cash both in good and bad times, if it is run properly, there can be greater monetization opportunities. And even if it doesn't yield superior returns, shareholders can derive satisfaction from the fact that they own a piece of Indian cricket and that their money is invested in an organization whose health is important for their own well-being.

Maybe finally, the tag 'Board of Controversies and Compromises in India' can be removed.

21

MUDGAL'S FINDINGS

The Mudgal Committee Report didn't just come down on Meiyappan, Kundra and the other accused. It also came down heavily on the system, especially on the police, pointing out cover-ups and suspect actions which had stymied investigations and, therefore, the revelation of truth. The committee stated that the betting syndicate today was operating virtually all through the country, more particularly in the mega markets of Delhi, Mumbai, Chennai, Indore, Ahmedabad, Jaipur, Goa, Pune, etc. Extensive use of electronic channels facilitated instant betting and settlement of dues. The betting organized by this huge structure involved a turnover of thousands of crore of rupees, which ultimately benefited known terrorists who routed the money to indulge in terror activities, posing a serious threat to national security.

Considering the seriousness of the threat, the committee pointed out that the response of the law enforcement agencies did not inspire confidence. It stated that various local law enforcement agencies were working independently, sometimes at cross purposes. Information conveyed from one agency to another was being viewed with suspicion, and leads were not being followed upon. Moreover, investigations by the Delhi Police and Mumbai Police remained confined to fringe players and to local bookies and fixers. Names of national and international players did come up in the course of the investigations, but this information was not investigated upon by the police.

Here are some important excerpts from the report:

(i) Chandresh Patel, according to the Delhi Police, is one of the key henchmen/fixers of Dawood Ibrahim. He was in direct contact with the bookies in Pakistan, and it was through him that the crime syndicate operated. It was through him that Dawood initiated spot-fixing by the Rajasthan Royals players. Curiously, Chandresh Patel, though known to the Mumbai Police to be a co-conspirator with Vindoo Dara Singh, is shown only as a witness and not as an accused in the Mumbai charge sheet.

(ii) The other significant case is of Mr Ramesh Vyas. The statement under Section 18 made by Ramesh Vyas under MCOCA in the Delhi case states that Ramesh Vyas was introduced to one Dr Javed Chautani, the alleged right-hand man of Dawood Ibrahim, by Chandresh Jain, also known as Jupiter, who facilitated his entry into the syndicate. Thereafter, with the approval of Dawood Ibrahim and Chhota Shakeel, Ramesh Vyas had gradually taken over the Mumbai turf, which had earlier been run by Firoz.

This statement of Ramesh Vyas was available to the Mumbai Police and was forwarded to them by the Delhi Police. The same is admissible as evidence in any criminal trial where Ramesh Vyas is an accused. Yet curiously, the Mumbai Police negate any connection between Ramesh Vyas and Dawood Ibrahim, and have denied before the Committee any knowledge that Ramesh Vyas was in charge of the betting operations of Dawood Ibrahim on the Mumbai turf. Ramesh Vyas, according to the Mumbai Police charge sheet, is projected to be only a bookie and an exchange operator. It is also pertinent in this connection to point out that the Q Branch CID, Chennai Police, which looks after internal security, already had Ramesh Vyas in its radar, and it has been disclosed before the Committee by Shri G. Sampath Kumar that the Chennai Police was aware that Ramesh Vyas was linked with Dawood.

The fact that the Mumbai Police did not accept the role of Dawood Ibrahim in the betting racket in Mumbai evinces that the Delhi Police and Mumbai Police are working at cross purposes in so far as the link to Dawood Ibrahim is concerned. In such a grave matter of national security pertaining to the involvement of a terrorist gang in running illegal *hawala* operations in the lucrative betting market in cricket, the two top police organizations, one of the political capital and other of the financial capital of India, cannot be permitted to work at cross purposes. It is not surprising that all the accused persons in both the cases are presently on bail and possibly back in business for the coming IPL season.

The investigating agencies have also been frustrated in their attempts, more often than not, in view of the absence of an appropriate substantial law on the matters of betting and fixing in sports. It is necessary that the law enforcement agencies find a level playing-field to eradicate corruption in cricket.

Role of Police

There are certain aspects of investigations conducted by various police authorities which have drawn the attention of this Committee and are required to be highlighted.

(i) *Role of Crime Branch, Mumbai Police*

A. In course of interception of phone calls between bookies, punters as well as foreign bookies in Pakistan, etc., the Mumbai Police had unearthed references made by bookies, etc., to connections of some Indian and foreign players with betting activities. Officers of the Mumbai Police indicated that investigations into such information were not carried out because there were no corroborations. It appears further from the deposition of the officers of the Mumbai Police that this information was not taken forward in connection with such names because, in view of the considered opinion of the Mumbai Police, the bookies were simply 'boasting' to increase their own influence. This position of the Mumbai Police is difficult to accept. The approach of the Mumbai Police appears very curious . . . more so keeping in mind the abrupt voluntary statement of the Mumbai Police before the Committee that their focus in the said investigation was Gurunath Meiyappan.

B. On being questioned by the Committee based on earlier media reports, it was admitted by the Mumbai Police that the iPad of Vindoo Dara Singh was seized and the deleted data therein was sought to be retrieved through forensic examination. This data would definitely reveal the various contacts and persons who were betting through Vindoo Dara Singh, who was already referred to in the CBI investigation report in 2000. Curiously, the Mumbai Police has not charged anyone else except Gurunath Meiyappan for laying bets in IPL matches through Ramesh Vyas, Vindoo Dara Singh and others. It is absolutely unbelievable that the Mumbai Police has failed to locate all such other persons who were involved in this betting racket. It is inconceivable such a huge betting syndicate would function for the benefit of only one person, Gurunath Meiyappan. The Mumbai Police has either been extremely naive in pursuing their investigation or they have deliberately not investigated the entire betting operations. Possibly, their statement that Gurunath Meiyappan was the focus is relatable to such shoddy investigation.

C. It is revealed from the investigation of the Delhi Police that Ramesh Vyas was the main kingpin of the betting operation maintained by Dawood Ibrahim in Mumbai. The Delhi Police claims that whatever information it had on Dawood's operations has been handed over to the Mumbai Police. The Mumbai Police, however, informed the panel that they have no conclusive material that Dawood Ibrahim was linked with the betting operations in Mumbai. The Mumbai Police admitted that protection by the underworld, i.e., muscle power, is essential to run an organized betting syndicate in Mumbai. The Mumbai Police failed to inform the panel as to which gang gave this protection to the betting operations in Mumbai. There is, therefore, cause for a distinct impression that for reasons not satisfactorily explained, the Mumbai Police was not willing to investigate the involvement of Dawood Ibrahim in the betting racket. In the entire charge sheet filed by the Mumbai Police, only one person who has laid bets has been charged as an accused, whereas all other accused are part of the betting syndicate. Evidently, the Mumbai Police is protecting lots of persons who were participants of betting activities through this syndicate. The quantum of bets allegedly made by Gurunath Meiyappan as per the transcripts will amount to a negligible fraction of the total betting in one IPL match, as disclosed by the Delhi Police and other available literature on betting in sports.

D. It may also be pointed out that information on proposed fixing of Mumbai Indians and Rajasthan Royals match on 15 May 2013 was available to the Mumbai Police on 12 May 2013 through the intercepted conversations of Asad Rauf, the umpire for the match. Yet, Asad Rauf was never detained by the Mumbai Police and was allowed to leave the country on 19 May 2013, after completing his pre-fixed assignments. Even a discreet lookout notice was not issued in the name of Asad Rauf. The extreme reluctance to address the issue of involvement of Dawood Ibrahim and the curious failure of the Mumbai Police to detain Asad Rauf, a Pakistani umpire, indicates possibilities which may require further investigation, keeping in mind the recent disclosure by the Home Minister of India that Dawood Ibrahim is presently based in Pakistan.

(ii) Role of the Special Cell, Delhi Police

A. The Special Cell of the Delhi Police has done a commendable job in bringing to light the involvement and control of the organized crime syndicate led by Dawood Ibrahim in the betting and fixing of cricket games in India. Having said that, it is necessary to deal with a few significant facts relating to the investigation conducted by the Delhi Police. The Delhi Police themselves claim that the four players were merely the tip of the iceberg. They had materials on record which suggested that there were definitely more players involved in spot/match-fixing. In fact, S. Sreesanth had given them information that three prominent players representing India were also involved with bookies and were getting flats and gifts from them. Curiously, the Delhi Police failed to investigate all such players whose names had cropped up during investigation. Only one such player was summoned for questioning by the Delhi Police. No further action was initiated. The transcripts of tape-recorded conversations between bookies, by the Crime Branch, Delhi Police, also mention two other Indian stars. The Delhi Police did not take all such information forward and explained their conduct by saying that they had only limited information and because they were aware that the bookies were generally in the habit of boasting. It is difficult to accept such explanation and in fact Mr Neeraj Kumar, formerly, Commissioner of Delhi Police stated in his deposition that further investigation should have been made as regard these references of bookies by players. If the tapes indicate criminality, it is the responsibility of the investigating agency to make proper investigations so as to ascertain the truth. The Delhi

Police did not record the statement of Mr Raj Kundra, either under Section 164 Cr.P.C. or under Section 18 of MCOCA. No explanation for this failure was forthcoming. After about 20 days, all information pertaining to Mr Raj Kundra was transmitted to the Commissioner of Police, Jaipur.

(iii) Role of Jaipur Police

A. The information pertaining to Mr Raj Kundra was forwarded by the Delhi Police to the Commissioner of Police, Jaipur, on 25 June 2013. No fruitful investigation was carried out in this connection by the Jaipur Police.

B. Mohammed Abdi had filed a written complaint in the matter of match-fixing between IPL teams, Chennai Super Kings and Rajasthan Royals, played on 12 May 2013 at Jaipur. The complaint was filed before the Court of Competent Jurisdiction, which forwarded the said complaint under Section 156(3) Cr.P.C. to the Jyotinagar Police Station wherein Case No. 269/2013 u/s 420/120B IPC was registered. No record has been placed before the Committee to show that any worthwhile investigation was carried out in this case as well and the serious allegations made therein possibly remain un-investigated.

C. The Committee desired to verify the interrogation report pertaining to Utham Jain, also known as Kitty, in connection with Q Branch CID Case No. 1/2013 u/S 120B 468,471 IPC and the Passports Act, 1967, as deposed by G. Sampath Kumar. The Superintendent of Police Q Branch CID (Internal Security) appeared before the Committee at 11:00 a.m. on 25 January 2014. She admitted that there was a file in the QBranch pertaining to the aforesaid case. The Committee was assured that the file would be produced at 4 p.m. by the Q Branch CID (Internal Security) and the investigating officer would be present. Thereafter, no one appeared before the Committee from Q Branch at 4 p.m. and the . . . file was not produced. There was no information and/ or any communication conveyed to the Committee either.

D. The incident is important because the then Superintendent of Police of the Q Branch who had submitted the interrogation report on 23 May 2013 had deposed before the Committee that Shri Utham Jain, also known as Kitty, had stated about a match-fixing deal concluded on 27 April 2013, which implicated one important Indian player, Gurunath Meiyappan and one Shri Vikram Agarwal. The non-production of the said interrogation report is therefore highly suspicious and seems to be deliberate.

E. Shri Utham Jain, also known as Kitty, after his interrogation by the Q Branch was handed over to the CBCID Branch of the Chennai Police. Apparently, no investigation on match-fixing was ever carried out by the Chennai Police and the officers who were privy to the contents of Kitty's statement under Section 161 of the Cr.P.C. were immediately transferred out from their respective positions. Curiously, the interrogation report of Kitty by the CBCID Branch of Chennai Police does not reveal anything about any deal on 27 April 2013.

F. This matter is of grave significance. There is a necessity for a further probe into the matter and the same may, therefore, be directed by the Honourable Supreme Court.

If Neeraj Kumar's investigations were successful in pointing out how deep the betting nexus was in the criminal world, then the Justice Mudgal Committee Report pointed out how ineffectual and compromised our corrections system was – be it the BCCI or the police themselves. What the report essentially did was to state on record something that everyone suspected, but nobody had the courage to say: all is not fine with cricket in India.

In fact, it is far from fine even today. The crisis that is facing cricket is different and far more sinister than anything it has faced before. Cricket, as it is played at present, no more resembles the game played by Sir Don Bradman or the one Neville Cardus wrote about. The romanticism associated with it is perhaps gone forever. Increasingly, in playing fields around the world, the music of a sweetly timed stroke is being replaced by the harsh cacophony of the ringing cellphones of bookies.

Instead of being worried about this state of affairs and rot in the game, what people at the helm today feel is only relief. None of the other teams were disqualified, no action was taken, six star-players against whom there was evidence have been shielded, and there was suspicion that more matches had been fixed other than the ones mentioned. It also appeared that the cops hadn't, for several reasons, done their jobs, and while we can hope that the investigative agencies will try and plug the holes pointed out by the Mudgal Committee, and all the conspirators in this drama, starting from Dawood and ending with BCCI's top management, will face the heat for their actions, it may eventually turn out to be a case of all for nothing.

For cricket today, it is a do or die situation as the credibility of the game has taken a beating. If the Mudgal Report proves to have no real repercussions and its suggestions remain only on paper, there is a very real danger that our future will look a lot like our present. Everything will go on as before: the BCCI will continue to act as its own boss; bets running into crores will be taken; conducive conditions to fix matches will prevail, and yet people will continue to watch these fixed matches on fields and at home, boosting ticket sales and TRPs; and the sponsors will continue laughing all the way to the bank. Some people may raise a voice of protest again, evidence may surface, new investigations will be started and committees appointed, and the BCCI may ban some players. But with time, the entire furore will die down once again. The bans will be lifted, ousted chiefs reinstated . . . More matches will be held, more money will be made. Another season will dawn, the game will go on. As the board officials are busy 'fixing' a new venue for a fresh IPL season, a courtroom drama gets scripted by the lawyers to ensure the perpetrators get away with minor punishments. And yes, among all other viewers, there will be Dawood, the police and careful bookies.

That sums up the story of Indian Cricket: the game must go on.

EPILOGUE

'If you play good cricket, a lot of bad things get hidden'
– Kapil Dev

The above words, then spoken with innocence and pure passion for the sport that literally drives the country, today resonate with a feeling of bitterness.

Cricket fans discovered for the first time that the underworld used betting syndicates to manipulate players, the game and partially if not fully, the outcome. Players were alleged to have fixed games, team owners were found to be involved in betting, cricket administrators were accused of protecting perpetrators and the highest judicial body in the country had to be approached to clean the richest game of the country.

However, the real question was why players got entangled into the lure of cheating and agreed to sabotage their game for 'meagre incentives' offered by a chain of betting syndicates linked to the most-wanted mobster, Dawood Ibrahim.

In strict legal terms, money is what money does. But illegally, money coupled with might does a lot more. The players may have been ignorant about this and not bothered to acknowledge the harsh reality of the various methods the underworld uses to cripple democratic economies from within, by fuelling illicit earnings into the legal economy.

The D-gang, led by Dawood Ibrahim, has mastered that art. Safe to say, Dawood's network that runs a parallel economy is more dreaded than terror groups at times because bad money eventually acts as a catalyst to worse crimes. Their synergy and ways of businesses help defeat the competition.

When we see the underworld, we look at contract killings, ransom, drug trafficking, weapons trade, extortions and racketeering. But this is only the surface; under this lies an enormous and illegally amassed economic power that is camouflaged and laundered until it becomes legal.

For over a decade, Dawood funneled his dirty money into Bollywood and cricket, the two most lucrative money spinners, eyeing the thrill apart from the mass recognition that he gained among his anti-social circuit. The gang was able to infiltrate into sports gambling circuits with the help of politicians and key social influencers, as they controlled liquidity in the market. Their exponential growth was guaranteed. Lending high and buying low was their first business strategy coupled with clout of fear. IPL was an easy breeding ground for corrupting the game and manipulating the highs and lows of cricket betting.

A lot of dirt was discovered during the investigation but the cricketers, especially those who knew about the illegal acts, go by the unwritten rule: "never corroborate what the prosecution claims unless it is proven by circumstantial and solid evidence". The courts have a challenging road ahead to pronounce the accused players as guilty due to the unsatisfactory evidence that finally appeared after a series of hearings.

'Eventually, the judiciary will have to bail the stumps from getting influenced from extraneous players.'

So far, successive cricketing managements, enforcement agencies, governments and cricket legends haven't succeeded in cleansing the game despite their attempts and claims. A large responsibility was entrusted to the Justice Lodha Committee to bring back respect for the game and institutionalize the management of cricket. The 159-page report recommends the legalisation of betting in the sport of cricket along with including BCCI under the RTI Act. The barring of any minister or government servant from holding office shows the firm stand taken by the committee. The proposal to introduce a CEO assisted by a team of six professional managers to handle the day-to-day non-cricketing affairs of the BCCI shows the intention to not only clean up the management but also bring about a definite change in the methods used. The committee members reckoned that a robust registration system along with separate committees chaired by only former players to handle issues related to selection, coaching, performance evaluation and umpiring would be in the best interest of all team members. However, the proposal to limit the autonomy of Indian Premier League (IPL) and to constitute separate governing bodies for the BCCI and the IPL so as to partially segregate their functioning, is bound to meet with some stern opposition.

For now, it looks like the judiciary is in the right direction to institutionalize the watchdogs of the sport. The series of recommendations of the Lodha Committee could prove to be the last nail in the coffin and hopefully, end an era of cricket, which neither the fans nor the players would want to visit.

●

Although the questions that the IPL scandal threw up about the sport mostly remain unanswered, one thing is certain after all the revelations: Betting on cricket is widespread, and perhaps the largest organized racket in the country in terms of monetary turnover and volume of transactions. According to rough estimates, the betting turnover for an ODI in any part of the world and being telecast live in India, can reach a couple of hundred crore rupees. IPL Season 6, which was at the heart of the fixing scandal, saw betting to the tune of a whopping Rs 400 billion!

This was not always so. Before the volume exploded to this level, there had been a lull in this activity. Before betting started approaching the borders of fixing where players took an active role in ensuring outcomes, the involvement of players was relatively passive. There were cases where players simply had to pass on information about team composition, probable results, the nature of the pitch, the weather, etc. But as technology grew and information and analysis became freely available to everyone, all top ringleaders of a betting syndicate knew that punters had begun to understand the game as much as the best cricketer or coach. Information could no longer be a leverage. To make more money, the next level had to be explored.

That's when the passive became the active and match-fixing as we now know it was born.

Match-fixing is a term coined by the media to describe instances wherein an individual player or group of players receive money individually or collectively to underperform. As more money entered the domain of speculation, it began acquiring a definite form of activity. The tricks of the game varied from 'fixing' players, to umpires (as in the case of Asad Rauf), to sometimes even instances where groundsmen were given money to prepare a pitch that suited the betting syndicate!

All of this led to an explosion in numbers. Betfair, one of the largest online betting sites born in the summer of 2000, coincidentally within a few weeks of the Hansie Cronje match fixing scandal, started to see huge bets from cricket. According to insiders, a top golf-tournament like the US Masters would attract bets worth 2–3 million pounds on Betfair.

For a smaller sport, with a very limited geography, cricket seems to do better. During the 2010 T20 World Cup in the West Indies, each match drew bets worth 3–4 million pounds. However, the IPL, which preceded the T20 World Cup by a few days, had seen betting amounting to over 12 million pounds per match on Betfair. Some of the matches, says an unimpeachable source, crossed 15 million pounds in bets. One site alone saw legal betting worth over a hundred crore rupees on one match. If there were even 20 more such sites, imagine the trade volumes they would generate. And this is just legal betting. Illegal betting is another ball game altogether.

A primary reason for the growth of this racket is the relatively liberal provisions of the Public Gambling Act in India. Even as it is debatable whether betting on cricket attracts provisions of this Act since cricket is theoretically a game of skill, the maximum punishment under this Act, for example in Delhi, for a first offence is imprisonment for six months and a fine of Rs 1,000; for subsequent offences, a maximum punishment of imprisonment for a year and a fine of Rs 2,000. Hence, for a bookie or a punter dealing in crores of rupees, the provisions of this Act are no major cause for concern. As an underworld personality who moved to big-time match-fixing put it, 'Betting and fixing has proved to be a far more lucrative business for us as compared to our traditional businesses of *supari* or contract killings, land-grabs or evictions. It leaves us cash-rich without a trace of blood on our hands, while there is some activity about *idhar ka maal udhar* (meaning, trading in drugs like cocaine, opium and heroin) depending on how well-placed you are both in the underworld as well as in the buyer's circuit. But all of this concerns a whole lot of people, including politicians, policemen, and civic officials. We end up paying almost 30 per cent of our income as tax because none of these activities, whether it is murder, land-grab or smuggling go unnoticed. It is exactly the opposite in betting and match-fixing. We are not on the radar unless we are caught. Besides, the law about gambling is so weak that many of us manage to escape with a fine of a mere thousand rupees.'

Legal experts say this is a grey area and has never been specifically addressed by a court. The Indian law on betting has evolved piecemeal since the first ban on gambling came into force in 1867 through the Public Gambling Act in what was then the United Provinces, East Punjab, Delhi and the Central Provinces. This act outlawed gaming houses, where cards, dice, tables or other instruments of gaming were kept or used for profit, but it permitted betting on games of mere skill. The law did not, however, define what constituted 'a game of skill'.

After Independence in 1947, all states had the freedom to set their own rules on gambling and betting; so today, betting laws differ from state to state. Even the police are not very clear about it. The Bengal Public Gaming Act, 1867, banned public gambling and owning a common gaming house, but permitted betting on horse races. The Bombay Prevention of Gambling Act, 1887, had similar provisions. Goa permits casinos, while Sikkim, since 2005, allowed gambling when monitored by the state. In 1996, a Supreme Court judgment on the legality of betting on horse racing in Tamil Nadu said that a game of mere skill was mainly and preponderantly a game of skill and ruled horse racing to be one. 'We have no hesitation in reaching the conclusion that horse racing is a sport that primarily depends on the special ability acquired by training,' the judgment said. 'It is the speed and stamina of the horse, acquired by training, which matters. Jockeys are experts in the art of riding. Between two equally fast horses, a better trained jockey can touch the winning post.' As a result, betting on horse racing doesn't count as gambling, the court adjudged. It only added that those wanting to place a bet must be within the confines of the racecourse.

Then previously, in 1968, the Supreme Court had found that the card game rummy was also a game of skill, because the fall of the cards had to be memorized and the building up of rummy required considerable skill in holding and discarding cards.

So, if horse racing and rummy are games of skill, what about sports such as cricket, which requires plenty of skill and training?

The chairperson of the probe panel appointed by the Supreme Court, Justice Mukul Mudgal, strongly felt that the law on betting is inconsistent. 'The betting law is paradoxical in India. You can bet on the skill of horses and skill of a jockey, but you can't bet on skills of a Sachin Tendulkar or a Sardar Singh,' Justice Mudgal said while addressing a conference at the Federation of Indian Chambers of Commerce and Industry (FICCI) on 'Regulating Sports Betting and Sports Law'. He called for legalizing betting in all sports, which would bring in tax and licensing revenue for the government. Given its size and complexity, FICCI has said legalization of sports betting in the Indian market could be a game changer with potential revenues slated to be upwards of nearly Rs 300,000 crore while generating employment, adding revenues to government coffers, and curbing money-laundering activities.

Sports betting has thus far been limited to horse racing and some state-organized lottery offerings, which come under the Lotteries Act of 1998. As India does not have a clear legal framework that recognizes sports betting, people rely on an illegal framework which puts them at risk on multiple fronts. If a tax rate of 20 per cent is prescribed, there is potential for around 200 million dollars in taxes for the government, said A. Didar Singh, Secretary General, FICCI. Most importantly, FICCI estimated that the government is losing up to USD 3.5 billion a year in taxable revenue through black-market betting on sport.

Globally, betting has evolved in different ways. In Austria, it is taxed at 28 per cent, while in the UK, it is taxed at 25 per cent; in places like Estonia and Lithuania, betting rates are much lower. In some instances, proceeds from betting are directed towards social issues, including funding for cultural or charitable causes, while also redirecting the money back to sports. China too has a sports lottery system, offered under the China Sports Lottery Administrative Centre. The revenue received through this lottery is first utilized to cover the lottery prizes and management funding, while the remainder is spent on public welfare.

In India, the sporting industry has called for the setting up of a committee, and eventually an Independent Regulatory Commission, which can conduct an in-depth study of sports gambling and arrive at solutions that eliminate the bookmakers. There is also a move to assess whether sports betting can be categorized as one involving skill-based games, which would put it on par with horse racing or poker.

The Indian Premier League to date is considered a hotbed of gambling. Indeed, thanks to its nature, all limited-over cricket is tailor-made for betting, which is why many countries have legalized it. However, India, which generates 80 per cent of the revenues in the game, has not made betting legal. The result, as the report by Justice Mudgal shows, is not just that betting is rife but also that there are attempts to fix outcomes. As a consequence, there are bound to be calls for different types of bans on the one hand, and for legalizing betting, on the other.

In sports betting, a price is announced and virtually no adjustments are made to it thereafter. This is unlike financial markets where prices of securities keep fluctuating based on new information. Thus, bookies are not market-makers in the way a broker in other financial markets is. The difference lies not in the fact that bookies in sports bet on final outcomes, but that they can bet on intermediate outcomes (though in some countries, the latter is also allowed so that you can bet on much shorter outcomes). The most important consequence of outcome betting on infrequently changing prices is that bookies tend to lose or gain (usually the latter) huge sums.

My own conclusion from this is that in cricket, betting tends to increase the temptation to fix matches. The only thing that the bookie has to choose from is the actual method of fixing. This can vary from passing on information for determining the price (benign wrongdoing) to bribing players to underperform (malignant wrongdoing). Much depends on what the aggregate losses of the bookies are through the tournament. If the gains are normal, only benign wrongdoing happens. But if the losses are huge, it turns malignant. So the key variable is to keep an eye on the profit levels of the bookmakers.

The only way this can be done is by legalizing betting in cricket. Otherwise, after periodic fuss, things tend to go back to business as usual where the chances of malignancy are higher. The problem, of course, is that those who gain the most from illegal betting perhaps also influence the course of government decisions the most.

Cricket, a vital part of the fabric of Indian society, today stands on the brink of ruin. The rampant corruption across all aspects of the game has made it no more than a money-making machine for a select few rather than the glue that binds together a billion people. It's increasingly beginning to appear that possibly the only way of salvaging this noble sport and restoring the faith of the people is by legalizing betting on the outcome.

ACKNOWLEDGEMENTS

This book is a result of a number of years of my personal research and immense support I received throughout. I would like to thank my journalist friends, a few of my close sources in the Indian law enforcement agencies and the financial world (who don't want to named) for sharing the necessary information when required.

Throughout the writing of this book, my fellow crime journalist at *Indian Express* and now an accomplished writer, Hussain Zaidi, has been a great force of encouragement.

I am grateful to the former police commissioner of Delhi, Neeraj Kumar, who took out the time from his schedule and shared his valuable feedback and also, to the director general of Maharashtra Police Datta Padsalgikar for his help in ascertaining some facts.

A special thanks to Chiki Sarkar, Abhijit Sathe, Ranjit Khomne, Abhijit Bramhanathkar, Shishir Prasad, Sharan

Saikumar, Saloni Lakhia and all my friends who helped me cross-check and collate facts and for actively participating in the making of this book. Many thanks to Kanishka Gupta and Avneet Kaur, who kept patience with my erratic writing schedules. Thanks to Prasun Chatterjee, the book is seeing the light of the day.

Without my wife Meghana Samant's insight portions of this book may have remained incomplete. A big thank you!

I have tried my best to give the exact information in the book, I apologize if some of the portions are not updated with the recent developments. The writing of this book has been a long process accompanied with long gaps. I hope you all enjoy reading it!

NOTES

Prologue

1. https://www.mid-day.com/articles/ipl-chargesheet-revealed-dawood-s-bookies-haggled-on-the-phone-with-bhai-showing-the-way/226505

2. https://www.news18.com/cricketnext/news/ipl-spot-fixing-scandal-how-it-unfolded-667489.html

3. https://timesofindia.indiatimes.com/news/BCCI-suspends-5-cricketers-for-IPL-spot-fixing/articleshow/13156492.cms

4. Reported in the past as encounters in pro-government press and assasinations by neutral media.

5. Intelligence dossiers maintained by the agencies and journalists for over last two decades.

6. https://timesofindia.indiatimes.com/sports/new-zealand-in-india-2016/top-stories/NDA-stopped-match-fixing-probe-Neeraj-Kumar/articleshow/27039594.cms

Chapter 1

1. https://www.indiatoday.in/india/north/story/dawood-ibrahim-javed-miandad-visa-issue-d-company-chhota-rajan-150919-2013-01-06

2. http://newsmobile.in/articles/2014/11/21/the-d-sultan/

3. Told to the author as journalist in those days.

4. https://www.news18.com/news/india/palatial-house-parties-prostitutes-dawoods-life-in-pakistan-1234711.html

5. https://www.news18.com/news/india/palatial-house-parties-prostitutes-dawoods-life-in-pakistan-1234711.html

6. In Pakistani media.

7. As reported in many media reports and Indian intelligence dossiers.

8. https://www.mid-day.com/articles/when-dawood-ibrahim-entered-the-indian-team-s-dressing-room-in-sharjah-in-1987/238130

9. https://timesofindia.indiatimes.com/sports/new-zealand-in-india-2016/top-stories/Dawood-entered-Indian-dressing-room-in-1986-offered-cars-to-players-Vengsarkar/articleshow/24822450.cms

10. https://www.tribuneindia.com/2002/20020203/spectrum/main1.htm

11. https://www.theaustralian.com.au/sport/opinion/frightened-and-confused-young-pakistani-mohammad-amir-trapped-by-the-underworld/news-story/2491f34150e34ab33008982c12826f26

12. https://www.bbc.com/news/world-asia-15576065

13. https://www.bbc.com/news/world-asia-15576065

14. https://www.smh.com.au/world/the-dark-underbelly-of-world-cricket-20070323-3vj.html

15. https://www.dawn.com/news/1016021

16. Intelligence sources.

Chapter 2

1. From police records.

2. Information compiled by police and journalists. This knowledge of betting known among journalists – me being one of them.

3. Witnessed by the author.

4. https://www.thehindu.com/todays-paper/tp-national/tp-newdelhi/you-cant-judge-a-bookie-by-the-cover/article4764454.ece

Chapter 3

1. This was the first visible appearance – pictures appeared in the media.

2. https://www.outlookindia.com/magazine/story/on-the-company-account/218798

3. https://timesofindia.indiatimes.com/interviews/Bhai-doesnt-want-haram-money-from-betting-Chhota-Shakeel/articleshow/20217827.cms

4. Widely reported in media – sourced information from cops and bookies.

5. https://www.topnews.in/law/all-matchfixers-are-answerable-dawood-ibrahim-claims-top-pak-bookie-225992

6. Information taken from police records.

7. From official police charge sheet.

Chapter 4

1. https://www.thehindu.com/todays-paper/tp-national/tp-newdelhi/you-cant-judge-a-bookie-by-the-cover/article4764454.ece

2. https://economictimes.indiatimes.com/news/politics-and-nation/ipl-spot-fixing-sunil-bhatia-also-fixed-matches-of-rebel-iclsays-police/articleshow/20210005.cms

3. An orginal chart is given on the placements of the bookies, etc. – the pyramid is a picture of how the flow happened from the highest authority in the pyramid like hierarchy of bookies, punters fixers, etc.

Chapter 5

1. https://www.indiatoday.in/india/north/story/ajit-chandila-ipl-spot-fixing-booking-betting-cricket-164019-2013-05-22

2. https://www.hindustantimes.com/delhi-news/transcripts-of-tapped-conversations-between-players-bookies/story-ETeWq2jOf86Nr1hSGGIndL.html

Chapter 6

1. https://www.thehindu.com/sport/cricket/ipl2013/the-tale-of-jiju-janardanan/article4721594.ece

2. https://sports.ndtv.com/indian-premier-league-2013/ipl-6-the-sreesanth-story-from-perfect-seam-to-spot-fixing-1536565

3. https://www.mid-day.com/articles/ipl-chargesheet-revealed-when-sreesanth-lost-his-cool-over-a-mobile/226507

4. https://www.ndtv.com/india-news/what-sreesanth-did-according-to-delhi-police-522390

5. https://www.mid-day.com/articles/ipl-chargesheet-revealed-when-sreesanth-lost-his-cool-over-a-mobile/226507

6. https://www.outlookindia.com/newswire/story/cops-recover-rs-55-lakh-paid-to-sreesanth-by-bookies/799409

Chapter 7

1. https://www.thehindu.com/news/national/bookies-approached-three-more-ipl-players/article4724015.ece

Chapter 8

1. https://economictimes.indiatimes.com/news/politics-and-nation/ipl-spot-fixing-case-rajasthan-royals-player-siddharth-trivedi-becomes-witness/articleshow/20370898.cms

2. https://timesofindia.indiatimes.com/interviews/Harmeet-Singh-says-Chandila-tricked-him-into-meeting-bookies/articleshow/21943502.cms

3. https://www.firstpost.com/sports/ipl/ankeet-chavan-is-a-chawl-boy-at-heart-lawyer-806339.html

Chapter 9

1. http://www.rediff.com/cricket/report/ipl-sreesanth-arrested-on-spot-fixing-charges/20130516.htm

2. http://www.espncricinfo.com/indian-premier-league-2013/content/story/636177.html

3. https://www.cricbuzz.com/cricket-news/57550/i-am-a-cricketer-not-a-terrorist-chandila

4. https://timesofindia.indiatimes.com/news/It-was-a-bolt-from-the-blue-Srinivasan-on-IPL-spot-fixing/articleshow/20086773.cms

5. Taken from police sources.

Chapter 10

1. http://www.espncricinfo.com/ci/content/story/654219.html

2. https://www.indiatoday.in/magazine/sport/story/20000417-police-claim-hansie-cronje-and-teammates-fixed-matches-but-the-south-africans-deny-charge-777369-2000-04-17

3. http://www.espncricinfo.com/ci/content/story/84318.html

4. http://www.espncricinfo.com/southafrica/content/story/84263.html

5. https://timesofindia.indiatimes.com/Match-fixing-googly-leads-to-diplomatic-row/articleshow/158328998.cms

6. https://www.telegraphindia.com/1000409/front_pa.htm

7. http://www.espncricinfo.com/ci/content/story/654219.html

8. Commented by the state officials.

9. https://www.thehindu.com/2000/06/15/stories/0215000l.htm

10. https://m.rediff.com/sports/2000/apr/20afp.htm

11. https://m.rediff.com/sports/2000/apr/20afp.htm

12. http://www.espncricinfo.com/ci/content/story/84318.html

13. https://www.thehindu.com/thehindu/2000/04/16/stories/0716028d.htm

14. https://www.theguardian.com/sport/2000/jun/08/cricket8

15. http://www.espncricinfo.com/ci/content/story/654219.html

16. https://www.theguardian.com/sport/2003/aug/03/cricket.features

17. https://www.theguardian.com/sport/2007/jul/01/cricket.features

18. http://www.espncricinfo.com/ci/content/story/84318.html

19. http://www.espncricinfo.com/match-fixing-anniversary/content/story/464111.html

Chapter 11

1. http://www.espncricinfo.com/ci/content/story/84318.html

2. http://www.espncricinfo.com/ci/content/story/84318.html

3. https://www.iol.co.za/sport/hero-hansie-could-save-cricket-51740

4. https://www.thehindu.com/thehindu/2000/05/07/stories/0107000d.htm

5. www.espncricinfo.com/ci/content/story/84318.html

6. http://www.espncricinfo.com/ci/content/story/84528.html

7. www.espncricinfo.com/ci/content/story/84318.html

8. https://gulfnews.com/sport/cricket/being-captain-of-india-is-not-easy-says-azharuddin-1.216817

9. https://www.thehindu.com/2000/04/21/stories/07210285.htm

10. https://www.thehindu.com/2000/06/16/stories/01160003.htm

Chapter 12

1. https://www.thehindu.com/2000/11/01/stories/01010006.htm

2. https://www.thehindu.com/thehindu/2000/11/03/stories/0203000a.htm

3. https://www.thehindu.com/thehindu/2000/11/03/stories/0203000a.htm

4. http://m.rediff.com/cricket/2000/nov/01full13.htm

5. http://m.rediff.com/cricket/2000/nov/01full13.htm

6. http://m.rediff.com/cricket/2000/nov/01full13.htm

Chapter 13

1. http://m.rediff.com/cricket/2000/nov/01sachin.htm

2. http://www.rediff.com/cricket/2006/oct/15azhar.htm?zcc=rl

Chapter 14

1. https://www.pressreader.com/india/hindustan-times-delhi/20140211/282419872146696

2. Mentioned in police remand application.

3. http://www.espncricinfo.com/pakistan/content/story/675081.html

4. https://timesofindia.indiatimes.com/life-style/spotlight/Leena-Kapoor-post-the-Asad-Rauf-controversy/articleshow/20859755.cms

5. https://www.dailypioneer.com/todays-newspaper/ill-be-happy-to-face-icc-probe-rauf.html

Chapter 15

1. https://timesofindia.indiatimes.com/news/Three-leading-bookies-of-Jaipur-were-in-touch-with-Vindu/articleshow/20218671.cms

2. https://timesofindia.indiatimes.com/videos/sports/t20/IPL-spot-fixing-Gurunath-Meiyappan-Vindoo-Dara-Singhs-voice-samples-match/videoshow/44925174.cms

3. https://www.thehindu.com/news/national/vindumeiyappan-call-transcripts/article5176486.ece

4. http://www.dailymail.co.uk/indiahome/indianews/article-2329263/Police-probe-phone-records-100-calls-texts-linking-Srinivasans-son-law-Meiyappan-Vindoo.html

5. http://www.espncricinfo.com/india/content/story/679413.html

Chapter 16

1. https://www.indiatvnews.com/sports/cricket/dhoni-raina-among-six-capped-players-named-in-mudgal-report-10635.html

Chapter 17

1. https://www.cricketcountry.com/news/shilpa-shetty-placed-bets-in-ipl-umesh-goenka-to-delhi-police-27562

2. https://indianexpress.com/article/news-archive/web/raj-kundra-and-shilpa-shetty-both-bet-say-police/

3. https://timesofindia.indiatimes.com/news/Raj-Kundra-confesses-to-betting-in-IPL-Delhi-Police/articleshow/20457677.cms

4. https://www.indiatvnews.com/sports/cricket/raj-kundra-faces-rr-suspension-police-waits-for-evidence-8271.html

5. https://www.indiatoday.in/india/story/raj-kundra-shilpa-shetty-ipl-ipl-spot-fixing-delhi-police-raj-kundra-twitter-165774-2013-06-06

6. https://timesofindia.indiatimes.com/news/Shilpa-Shetty-denies-role-in-IPL-betting-cops-say-Raj-Kundra-bet-on-his-team/articleshow/20462033.cms

7. https://www.business-standard.com/article/beyond-business/man-of-the-match-112072100061_1.html

8. https://www.news18.com/cricketnext/videos/neeraj-on-raj-614205.html

Chapter 18

1. https://www.bollywoodpapa.com/read-one-sided-love-story-madhubala-gangster-haji-mastan/

Chapter 19

1. https://economictimes.indiatimes.com/news/politics-and-nation/sahara-group-withhold-bank-guarantee-because-of-bccis-betrayal-of-trust/articleshow/24764708.cms

Chapter 20

1. https://www.indiatoday.in/sports/cricket/story/is-bcci-above-the-law-asks-kirti-azad-172007-2013-07-29

